LONDON
REVEALED

LONDON REVEALED

JOHN FREEMAN

Text by JOHN FREEMAN *and* PETER DORMER

LITTLE, BROWN AND COMPANY

To Teresa,
Who showed me the door
For Sue,
Who gave me the key

A Little, Brown Book

© Little, Brown 1992

Photographs © John Freeman 1989

First Published in Great Britain in 1989
by Macdonald & Co (Publishers) Ltd
London & Sydney

This paperback edition first published
in 1993 by Little, Brown

**British Library Cataloguing in
Publication Data**
Freeman, John
  London Revealed
  1. London, buildings, Interior design
  I. Title II. Dormer, Peter
  747.22'1

  ISBN 0 316 90727 8

Filmset by August Filmsetting, Haydock,
St. Helens

• Printed and bound in Italy by Graphicom SRL,
Vicenza

Senior Commissioning Editor Joanna Lorenz
Senior Art Editor Philip Lord
Production Controller Marguerite Fenn
Text Peter Dormer of Design Analysis
International
Text Editor James Harrison
Layout Designer Andy Smith

Little, Brown and Company (UK) Ltd,
165 Great Dover Street
London
SE1 4YA

*Pictured on page one: the Lord
Mayor in residence at Mansion
House (see page 142).*

*Pictured on the frontispiece:
Blackburn House (see page 204).*

Contents

CONTENTS

Introduction

EW OF US get the chance to see the full richness and diversity of London's interiors, partly due to lack of awareness about many of the Capital's treasures, and partly because some are either private or very exclusive. I feel these are treasures that should be shared, with visitors and those who may never visit London as well as amongst those of us who live here.

London is a city of interiors. It is not the easiest place for outside living; the parks of course, are pretty, and some of the thoroughfares are grand but both the weather and the general grey demeanour of the London street militate against continental-style street living. One exception to this rule is perhaps London's famous 'street fashion' – our ostentatious punks and others who parade in orange or green hair and get their pictures snapped by the tourist.

However, Londoners are on the whole a secretive lot; unlike, say the Dutch (with whom the British have much in common) the Londoner does not like to open his home to the public. In Amsterdam those tall thin houses have large windows blazing with light, unshuttered and opening up the rooms within to the street. Even the prostitutes in Amsterdam sit in little windows (in Soho their existence is more furtive). The exteriors of London's buildings, too, are often uniform and unprepossessing, with little to indicate the fantastic decoration and detail that may exist within.

Once you are actually inside London there is a wealth of real art and invention to delight the eye and uplift the heart. Nor is it only the older London buildings which contain beautiful and eccentric interiors. There are 20th-century homes, shops, restaurants and offices that are just as appealing, sometimes if only because of their diversity and sheer bloody-minded energy. I think that the quality of decoration and architecture which this book celebrates corrects the seemingly general view that London has been ruined architecturally. This, in many of the examples revealed here, is patently not the case.

It was in the late-Victorian splendour of Wyndham's Theatre that I had the idea of photographing London from inside, and I knew that I wanted a mixture of interiors – private as well as public, and humble as well as grand.

When I walk around houses like the Tower House or Debenham House or Leighton House I am amazed and delighted by the humour, the humanity and the cleverness with which everyday emotions and ideas and the small change of day-to-day living are symbolised in carving, narrated in decorated tiles, or dramatised in mosaic or mouldings. The late 19th century and early 20th century have as much to teach us as the much-respected classical explorations of the late 18th century.

Learning from the past, discovering and rediscovering earlier architectural styles and the values and ideas they represented is not only an honourable architectural practice, it is unavoidable. Architecture and the applied arts are communal activities. Thus we see architects as different as Pugin, Barry, Robert Adam, Wren and Inigo Jones

revitalising historical precedents. Sometimes the introduction or re-introduction of an architectural style was a
matter of fierce ideological or cultural debate. Inigo
Jones appeared to have deplored the 'provincialism' of
English life and sought his inspiration from the Italian
architect Palladio. Pugin, on the other hand, was at one
with the Victorians who were equally fierce in their commitment to Gothic, considered by some to be a more
English (and patriotic) style.

In this century architecture and interior design have
nearly come full circle. In the early 1900s style was the
comfortable, expansive assured excess of Edwardian and
Art Nouveau embellishment. This was in fact soon chal-
lenged by the Edwardians themselves – we forget how
exciting modernism was to the Edwardians, to novelists
and storytellers like H. G. Wells, for example. The
excitement of machinery, of electricity and, above all, of
flying caught the imagination of architects and designers.
There was a desire to express modernity (even Edwardian Christmas cards sometimes showed Father Christmas flying in on a bi-plane). Consequently, a harsher,
plainer, more machine-smooth, machine-efficient modern classicism emerged. A leading exponent of this was
Charles Holden, who by the 1930s was London's most
visible modernist.

But styles never evolve smoothly. Wedged between
the grace of Edwardiana and the flowering of modernism
was Art Deco – that curious mixture of the organic and
the geometric. What was striking about the inter-war
period was the genuine diversity of style – clients could
ask for anything and get it.

However, in the domestic domain, the same period
saw a great increase in uniformity. The rapid expansion
of the suburbs was based on the principle of more of the
same. And after the Second World War the principle of
uniformity became endemic. Although the hiatus that
exists in this book between 1940 and 1980 is not deliberate (I never planned the book to have such an emphasis),
looking back I recognise it was, in fact, inevitable.

I am attracted to eccentricity, change, individuality,
symbolism, metaphor and decoration. Not until the
1980s do I really find these characteristics again – at the
point where 'modernism' has given way to what the critics call 'post-modernism'. Post-modernism is not a
single style; it is rather an umbrella description beneath
which there is a variety of styles, ideas and goals. It may
be that in twenty years time this period will be seen as a
transitionary one as architects and designers and their
clients feel their way towards decoration and building
which express ideas and values that ordinary intelligent
people delight in: nature, sex, civic and religious values,
fancy, myth and invention. One might argue that too
often clients force architects to compromise their
designs: English clients can too often, like English people
generally, prefer the cosy to the rigorous. Nostalgia (as
opposed to a scholarly understanding of the past) is an
English disease afflicting not only architecture but culture generally.

The late 20th century is a cruel time for architects:
buildings, especially public or commercial buildings, are
technically much more complex than their predecessors
(they talk, nowadays, of the 'intelligent' building). And

cost constraints, the need to make less do more and more efficiently, threaten every effort at creating architecture and design that pleases the public. Ours is also an age which does not believe in one dominant set of values and so it is harder than ever to make buildings that mean something positive. Time, of course, makes most passable efforts pleasantly familiar; familiarity makes things comfortable. We must be wary of over-judging too hastily things that appear odd.

This is a celebratory book and I hope that the reader will find much that is pleasurable – one of my intentions in taking the photographs was to give you the opportunity (which close-up photographs so ably provide) of taking a closer look at some of London's inner treasures. Nothing can take the place of an on-site visit but on the other hand the photograph does afford one the chance of a closer, more leisurely scrutiny. I hope too that the views expressed in this book will be accepted for what they mostly are – personal opinions based on the research of many people, whose work I freely and gratefully acknowledge and whose own books are warmly commended to you.

As I write HRH The Prince of Wales is again in the news condemning the beastliness of 20th-century architecture; it is a small but pleasant irony for me that the interior which set me off, Wyndham's, was once a favourite of a former Prince of Wales.

John Freeman
London 1989

RIGHT *Wyndham's Theatre, Charing Cross Road (see also page 64). This is the interior that was the inspiration for the book.*

CHAPTER ONE

The Grand Scale

OPPOSITE *In 1854 Sydney Smirke added the Reading Room of the British Library to the British Museum (designed by his brother Robert Smirke). Libraries are designed to encourage the ideals of scholarship and speculation. Like the architecture of the best churches their interiors should encourage us to disdain the mediocre.*

GRANDNESS IS NOT DEFINED by a single style, nor is it the product of mere size. A small interior can be grand when the proportions are right and if there is a sense of power tempered with maturity. Grand is not simply *theatrical* – a theatrical event captures the mood of the moment whereas the *grand* manner conveys continuity. Inigo Jones founded the English classic school of architecture and helped English architecture become grand. He learned the science of harmonious proportions from the Roman architectural theorist Vitruvius, and from studying the buildings of Roman Renaissance architect Alberti and the great 16th-century architect Palladio in Italy. Monarchs and the Church demanded grandness to symbolise the maturity of their power but, as the co-operative ventures of science and art grew, so too did secular architecture, which became capable of symbolising civic responsibility, art, science and the grandeur of learning. The splendid Reading Room (see facing page), with its wide dome, conveys this spirit of enlightenment.

ABOVE *Lancaster House (see page 20) has foundations by the 19th-century British architect Robert Smirke, but the main design is by his contemporary Benjamin Wyatt (Smirke, however, completed the task). The central hall and stairway was designed by the architect of the Palace of Westminster – Sir Charles Barry.*

Now a Government conference and hospitality centre it is impressive but stuffy – it has the atmosphere of crushed velvet. Humour is missing, but can governments laugh?

NATWEST BANK, BISHOPSGATE

THE NATIONAL WESTMINSTER BANK stands out architecturally in London with its modern tall tower in Bishopsgate. It was designed by Richard Seifert who has changed the face of London in this century as much as Wren wrought his architectural changes in the 17th century. The 600-foot tower – Britain's tallest office block in the 1980s – is the centre of the bank's international business, but the old headquarters of the bank, nestled well below, have been refurbished as the National Westminster Bank Conference Centre.

The Bishopsgate building, once described as a 'richly decorated Corinthian pavilion' was designed by John Gibson and it opened in January 1866 as No 15 Bishopsgate. It almost received a death sentence in 1959, but fortunately the bank's plans to demolish it for redevelopment were quashed. Justly so, for the elegant grandeur of the hall is a historic reflection of the nature of 19th-century banking transactions.

The refurbishment of the building into a conference centre has necessitated some adaptation – the installation of new ventilation systems and heating. But the upgrading of the interior for the requirements of the late 20th century has been carried out unobtrusively. The lighting has been given a theatrical cast through the installation of chandeliers and the addition of fluorescent tubes above the cornice. One of the bonuses of the refurbishment was the opportunity it gave for clearing the main banking hall of the screens, counters and other equipment demanded by modern banking. Thus the hall is now seen as John Gibson himself would have seen it.

One of the interesting aspects of Victorian architecture is that civic and commercial buildings (such as banks) would be decorated with designs and images that symbolised the institution's work. Thus on the exterior of the building the function is announced through visual imagery: panels representing the arts, commerce, science, manufactures, agriculture, navigation and shipbuilding. Inside at the end of the hall we see four panels representing the production of gold and coinage and the association with banking. The opulence of the decoration – the emphasis upon gold – and the *gravitas* of the marble pillars symbolise the weight and the richness of the bank, and convey by implication the qualities of durability that customers like to associate with their bank.

ABOVE *The 1939–45 War Memorial tablet.*

RIGHT *Marble pillars finished off in the Corinthian manner and embellished with gold leaf.*

ABOVE *The 1914–18 War Memorial tablet.*

OPPOSITE *John Gibson was a pupil of Sir Charles Barry, architect of the Houses of Parliament. Gibson's use of the delicately traced glass domes is a light relief both metaphorically and literally.*

THE GUILDHALL

ONE OF THE CHARACTERISTICS of an old city is that inner and outer do not always match up: just as you may be surprised to discover an Adam interior inside the late 20th-century Lloyd's building (see page 39), so too you might be pleasantly deceived by the Guildhall's partly Gothic exterior – because inside we are given a quasi-Medieval treat.

The Guildhall has a lively history. The current building began life in 1411 under Henry IV, and on completion stood until the Great Fire of 1666. The walls remained but not much else. The building was reconstructed. In 1788-89 George Dance the Younger, who introduced many of London's first 'circuses' and 'crescents' and whose famous pupil was Sir John Soane, created the Gothic front porch. It is a rather tantalising mix because it is sprinkled with both Greek and Indian touches. And then the Victorians had a go.

The Victorians are sometimes blamed for insensitive restoration and a tendency to rebuild things in their own image, but under the direction of J.B. Bunning and then Horace Jones (City Architects) the Guildhall was restored to what was believed to be its Medieval style. Photographs of the interior created by Horace Jones show a romantic but thoroughly enjoyable piece of Medieval theatre, but experts still debate whether the restoration was authentic or not. Not that authenticity alone recreates a building's original spirit.

On the 29th December 1940 the building was bombed out. Sir Giles Scott was put in charge of the reconstruction (his son taking over in the 1960s when Giles died). Giles Scott, grandson of noted architect Sir George Gilbert Scott (see page 80) disputed a number of Jones's decisions and in particular he had strong views on the construction of the roof. The present roof is the fifth one to span the Medieval space. The hall today is in the very same space it was in 1411 and there are seven Medieval columns to the north and seven to the south. Some of these columns were damaged in the Great Fire and they had to be rebuilt around their tops – you can tell by the fact that the colour in the stone changes. The large east and west windows are, apparently, more or less as they were originally, although there have been continuous repairs to the mullions and transoms.

The Guildhall is a centre of civic affairs and consequently it is like a municipal mantelpiece – just as one collects and displays objects of personal or sentimental significance on a mantelshelf at home so, gradually, the Guildhall has become the site of statues, plaques, heraldic shields and commemorative monuments. The names of the Livery Companies – the Mercers, Grocers, Drapers, Fishmongers and so on – connect the ordinary life of the citizen with his or her rulers. Both are here.

So, this is a grand but friendly building: it retains that favourite English atmosphere – mellowness.

ABOVE *Bronze statue of Sir Winston Churchill completed by Oscar Nemon in 1958.*

BELOW *Magog (shown here) and Gog are two giants who have greeted monarchs and citizens for centuries. These statues are modern (the earlier versions being destroyed in 1940).*

ABOVE *Sir Giles Scott's roof – the bold pattern of plain arch and ribbed wooden roof is a masterpiece of decorative rectitude.*

RIGHT *Jewel-like shields of the livery companies.*

OPPOSITE *The restoration of the roof of the Great Hall began in 1953. The stone arches of the new roof continue the lines of the ribs of the columns. All the new stone work was toned and tooled to match the Medieval walls.*

THE GRANADA, TOOTING

PLANNERS AND ARCHITECTS or even worse, local politicians often talk about 'buildings for people' and 'people's palaces'. But this extraordinary cinema – The Granada, Tooting – really is a people's palace.

It opened in 1931 and has seating for 4,000 people, and all the interior decoration was designed by Theodore Komisarjevsky, a stage set designer who studied architecture in Russia and Germany and who was, for a short while, married to Dame Peggy Ashcroft. Of course, it is kitsch – if you accept the idea that kitsch occurs whenever a lot of different styles and artefacts are raided and put together in a melange. But as we see throughout this book, examples of pure styles are rare, and some of the best interiors show a multiplicity of influences. Moreover, one can hardly call this cinema a melange. On the contrary it is a well composed interior with a series of visual rhythms – the interior is like a pool with ripples flowing from a still centre.

Like many old picture houses, it couldn't withstand the competition of television and became unprofitable. Fortunately it has escaped the fate of being destroyed or redeveloped and retains much of its original splendour.

The sheer size of the Granada, and the elaborate nature of the design with its rounded and pointed arches, produce an almost cathedral-like quality. In fact, at its peak the cinema must have seemed a veritable temple of entertainment. It undoubtedly deserves its preservation, but its current use as the largest bingo hall in the country gives some sense of an abandoned faith, while the lines of one-armed bandits along its walls add an irreverent reminder of Las Vegas.

The style is Gothic with a flavour of Moorish influence. It is full of fakes and illusions, but then it is designed to be like a dream. You can almost visualise it appearing and then disappearing as the lights come on for an interval and then down for the reeled news and then up again, then down for the B film and so on. It is like being in a painting or, perhaps, a hologram.

Much has been written of the cleverness, the detailing, the artifice of modern 'people's palaces' such as the vast shopping malls and hypercentres, but none of them match the splendour of this interior. Again it is a matter of confidence. Modern interior designers are far too busy being worried about what their peers and the design press will say about them – their work is too full of 'quotations' and 'ironic details'. No one has pulled off a stunning pastiche like this for years.

ABOVE *The line of the arches is wild, it swoops and curls in an exaggerated copy of Gothic – it is Disneyesque architecture which owes much to the fairground tradition. This is folk art – vulgar but skilled.*

LEFT *The plaster mouldings are not crude, but rather serviceable – after all, no-one was expected to stand on the stairs examining them as if they were in a museum.*

OPPOSITE *The theatre is decorated with murals that suggest Arthurian legends – the characters float, all is ephemeral. A poor man's Veronese.*

APSLEY HOUSE

APSLEY HOUSE IS ALSO KNOWN as No 1 London or the Wellington Museum. The house was originally designed by Robert Adam in the period 1775-78 but it was altered and extended in 1828-29 by the brothers Benjamin and Philip Wyatt. Some of the interiors remain as Adam designed them – these include the drawing and portico rooms. The Waterloo Gallery (this was the house of the 1st Duke of Wellington) is by Benjamin Wyatt.

The Waterloo Gallery is obviously militaristic and masculine, a room for pacing and posturing as well as displaying Wellington's collection of paintings of the period. Many of these paintings were spoils of war. There are three Rococo-style chimney pieces in yellow sienna; indeed, the gallery burns with gold. In fact the gallery was originally gold in its entirety – the current crimson being a later change by the 2nd Duke of Wellington.

The Dining Room is another masculine interior although it is plainer than the gallery. The vast mahogany table sits like an aircraft carrier in this space and supports a silver and silver-gilt service. This was a gift of Portugal.

The staircase greets you with a statue of Napoleon I which was carved by Antonio Canova. You might have fancied that Napoleon would be flattered by the powerful, athletic carving, but he disliked it – it failed to express what Napoleon felt was his calm dignity. In his hand Napoleon clutches the figure of Victory. History is full of irony. What is intriguing is why the British Government bought it. To gloat? It was given to Wellington by George IV – like a trophy head, it seems. Canova fared well from Napoleon's downfall, by being created a Marquess for recovering works of art from Paris after Napoleon's defeat.

The 18th century (the Duke of Wellington was born in 1769 and died in 1852) may have been genteel in its art and architecture but it is not notable for its kindness. The Duke's mother apparently remarked of him that he was ugly and 'fit food for powder'. Catherine Pakenham, Wellington's wife, died at Apsley House on April 24th, 1831 – after an unhappy and uncongenial 25-year marriage.

FAR LEFT *Statue of Napoleon by Antonio Canova, 1806. It is over 11 feet high and the British Government bought it for 66,000 francs.*

LEFT *The Waterloo Gallery contains a number of notable paintings by great contemporary artists of the period including Van Dyck, Jan Steen I, Jan van der Heyden and Sir Joshua Reynolds.*

OPPOSITE *The silver service on display in the Dining Room was made in the Military Arsenal at Lisbon from 1812 to 1816. Certain art historians single this out as the great monument of Portuguese Neo-Classical silver.*

LANCASTER HOUSE

ON THE OUTSIDE this building is somewhat plain but inside it is rich. This outer/inner duality reflects the manners of the early 19th century in which the aristocracy (old money) felt it clever to disguise what they really had and thus distinguish themselves from the *nouveaux riches* who worked on the principle of ostentation at all times. Lancaster House functions as a Government conference centre and also hosts a variety of receptions attended by members of the Royal Family and public dignitaries, often to welcome important representatives from other countries. It was built over a period of about 15 years, starting in 1825 on foundations laid down earlier by Robert Smirke, who also designed the London Museum (1824-7). The main design, however, is by Benjamin Wyatt.

Originally intended as the rebuilt home of the Duke of York, it suffered several delays through the deaths of first the Duke, and then the Marquess of Stafford who had subsequently bought the lease, renaming it Stafford House. It was not finished until the early 1840s under the instructions of yet another new owner, the 2nd Duke of Sutherland. His wife, Harriet, was a close friend of Queen Victoria who often visited as a guest and once said, 'I have come from my house to your palace'.

For many years the scene of lavish balls and a meeting place of politicians, it was sold in 1912 to Sir William Lever, later 1st Viscount Leverhulme, the soap and detergent entrepreneur who started Lever Bros. It was Leverhulme who renamed the building Lancaster House in honour of his native county.

The interior has a central hall and stair by Sir Charles Barry. It is Barry's hall and staircase which is the main attraction, described as 'one of the most impressive spatial experiences in London'. However, the interior as a whole offers another experience – the place is riddled with static electricity, a strange feature in a building used for Government hospitality.

Benjamin Wyatt sought to recreate the style of decorative art that characterised the reign of Louis XIV, and Benjamin Disraeli praised it by saying it was 'not unworthy of Vicenza'. The central hall has copies of paintings by Paolo Veronese, and the ambience is one of understated wealth with the gilded balustrade sparkling against the foil of the imitation marble columns. Paintings, including work by Guercino and Lorenzi, form an important part of Lancaster House's decoration.

ABOVE LEFT *The balustrades of the galleried landing are made from marble and polished granite.*

LEFT *This chased and gilded chimney piece is elaborated with veined marbles from Italy. It is in the Long Gallery, which formerly housed the collection of paintings that now form the basis of the National Gallery of Scotland.*

ABOVE RIGHT *A detail from the West Drawing Room, which has its original furnishings although the chairs, as with this one here, have been re-covered.*

OPPOSITE *The Music Room (a rather vulgar confection, nouveau riche even, with its gilding). The view through the door is towards the Grand Staircase.*

ABOVE *These paintings along the Grand Staircase (built in 1838 and considered by some to be the best staircase in England) are copies of paintings by Veronese. The wall surfaces are imitation marble.*

LEFT *In the West Drawing Room the ceiling panels represent part of the solar system.*

OSTERLEY PARK HOUSE

THE GRANDEUR of Osterley Park House, which was restyled by Robert Adam during the period 1761-80 for the banker Robert Child, begins with the Ionic portico – a severe beginning which is softened when you see the decorous under-surface. You are then led through the Entrance Hall, a room which is splendid in its coolness and bold in its decoration. The military trophy panels imply that such gracious surroundings are only for the brave or, as Mark Antony said, for when the task is done.

This Entrance Hall has more than a hint of Imperial Rome. But the use of the apse (one might call it an Adam signature) provides a touch of relief to the grandeur – it gives, in Adam's hands, a sense of civilised solace deriving from its enclosing form. But these apses are never 'cosy' – there is nothing Little Englander about Adam even at his most domestic. You may not be quite prepared for the variety of interiors that then follows – the Library Room, for example, has an enchanting ceiling of such colourful strength and delicacy that it has much in common with the elaboration of ceramic ware. Yet the scale of the composition is much more daunting than that posed by any bowl or vase. This is a sweet room, it is the gentler side to Adam's formal politeness. The Etruscan (or rather Greek) dressing room is almost over-elaborate – a *tour de force* combining complexity with great order. Just reflect on what dense chaos is created 100 years on from Adam when the Victorian bourgeoisie sought to create elaboration in their own homes. But then what becomes strikingly clear is the importance of not having too many things in a room, and then placing what things you do have very carefully. This is one of Adam's secrets – a

LEFT *The Etruscan Dressing Room with ceiling decoration by P. M. Borgnis and a roundel by Antonio Zucchi. Adam's inspiration for this room was fuelled by the figurative motifs decorating classical vases. This is one of four rooms by Adam and the only one surviving.*

ABOVE *The Tapestry Room: this room contains a set of tapestries woven by Jacques Nielson at the Gobelins tapestry works in Paris.*

careful integration of the furniture with the walls and the ceiling; he was a designer, and everything within the compass of a room was designed to fit, to complement or to reciprocate both the vocabulary of detail in the room and its overall composition. An Adam interior *directs* your very deportment.

Much of the furniture, but not the wall pieces such as the Etruscan furniture, was designed by cabinet makers commissioned by the owners. The craftsmen included William Linnell and Thomas Chippendale the Elder, whose name is synonymous with the Anglicised Rococo style. Such men designed in Robert Adam's Neo-Classical manner.

Robert Adam's contribution to British architecture, design and decoration is, obviously, very special. His body of work is the essence of what we perceive to be 18th-century grace and fastidiousness. But credit must go also to the craftsmen who carried out his designs. The development of such splendid and complicated buildings as Osterley Park House required a lot of skilled labour. Adam was in the hands of his craftsmen, and yet the order, harmony and consistency of effect inside Osterley Park House are a testimony to his organisation. At one stage his business employed 2,000 people. The senior craftsmen (cabinet makers, sculptors and decorative painters) in fact did rather well financially – and deservedly so.

ABOVE *The Library Room: the lyre-back chair is by John Linnell. Furniture makers like Linnell were well capable of designing their own Neo-Classical furniture – it would be misleading to read 'mute mechanical' for 'craftsman'.*

LEFT *The Drawing Room: this extraordinary ceiling is adapted from a drawing of a ceiling from a room at Palmyra, Syria.*

ABOVE *Fireplace and detail from fireplace in the Library Room. The delightful symmetry and naturalism of plaster work such as these putti present the archetypal logo of the 18th century. This plaster work was by Joseph Rose and Company.*

RIGHT *The Library Room, with furniture by John Linnell and bookcases by John Gilbert. The inset paintings are by Antonio Zucchi except those above the fireplaces which are by Giovanni Battista Cipriani – a pioneer of the 'Adam style' in decorative mural painting.*

THE ROYAL OPERA HOUSE

THE ROYAL OPERA HOUSE, Covent Garden, is the third such building on the site. It was designed by E.M. Barry, son of Sir Charles Barry the architect who, with A.W.N. Pugin, designed the Houses of Parliament (see page 113). Barry's building replaced one by Sir Robert Smirke which was burnt down in 1856. Smirke had in turn replaced a theatre designed by Edward Shepherd which, when it opened in 1732, was the most luxurious theatre ever built in London. Barry's building, which opened in 1858, was allegedly built in six months.

The Opera House is not placed in a prominent position, and although the great portico does its best to offer a sense of grand occasion it actually feels uncomfortably hemmed in. Behind the portico there is a frieze showing Comedy and Tragedy, which was designed by John Flaxman and comes from Smirke's original building.

Inside the auditorium one can see the influence of architect Sir John Soane (see page 68). The large shallow dome is certainly Soane-like and it is cleverly penetrated to create a third tier of seats. It is a very rich confection of gilded mouldings and garlands, with crimson velvet seating that can accommodate 2,141

opera buffs. However, it is also redolent of good old British saloon bar taste, which is quite at one with modern opera audiences who always seem about to bubble over either with exuberant pleasure or sheer disgust (in contrast with the less strident audiences at London's National Theatre) – the middle way finds no expression, and perhaps the decor reflects this.

Opera, which in the late 1980s is enjoying greater popularity and wider and bigger audiences than ever before, is extraordinarily expensive to produce and the Royal Opera House is heavily subsidised. Ticket prices have always been a problem. When the previous building was erected in place of the first opera house which burned down in 1808, the management put the prices up. This caused 61 nights of riots until the management gave in.

The theatre was shut during the two World Wars, when it was used both as a furniture repository and as a Mecca Dance Hall. It re-opened in 1946, with Ninette de Valois's Sadler's Wells ballet joining as the resident ballet company. Today, the Royal Ballet and the Royal Opera, granted their Royal Charters in 1956 and 1968 respectively, share equal honours in one of the world's finest and best-loved opera houses.

ABOVE *Detail of the gilded plaster mouldings which embellish the base of the dome.*

LEFT *This is not a view you are likely to see very often unless you take up ballet or opera singing since it is shot from the stage.*

OPPOSITE *The theatre opens up from the Gods like a great clam with the stage as its pearl.*

THE ROYAL ALBERT HALL

'Now, what i want is, Facts ... Facts alone are wanted in life.' So said Mr Gradgrind in Charles Dickens's satire of Victorian Britain *Hard Times*. The very Victorian Royal Albert Hall supplies plenty of these: it is 735 feet in circumference and can hold 8,000 people. The span of the roof is 219 by 185 feet, and the edifice holds six million bricks. And, as a newspaper description of the period aptly described it, 'The roof, which rests upon the inner wall, is a huge skylight, the frame-work resembling the ribs of a gigantic outspread umbrella.' It was opened in 1871 – designed by an engineer Lt-Colonel Scott of the Royal Engineers. It has been suggested that the idea of the single domed brick cylinder was originally nurtured by Gottfried Semper, a political refugee befriended by Prince Albert.

The impetus for the Hall came from the Prince Consort who was something of a designer himself (he co-designed Osborne House) and had successfully managed the Great Exhibition of 1851 at the Crystal Palace. Albert died while planning the South Kensington Exhibition in 1861, but the area, with its great museums, as well as the Royal Albert Hall, is a testimony both to his energies and to the philanthropic side of Victorian values.

The interior is a marvellously theatrical and a very adaptable space: it has hosted the grandest of classical concerts and the most plebeian of boxing matches. In its rich Victorian crimsonness the Royal Albert Hall has proved to be an impressive example of Victorian practicality and whimsy. Sadly, the Hall is now facing some problems with the exterior terracotta – a clay material with a tough skin and a soft heart.

FAR LEFT *The centrepiece of the space is the organ which stands 70 feet high, and the weight of the largest of its 10,000 pipes is awesome – over a ton apiece. Designed by Henry (Father) Willis it cost the then princely sum of £10,000 – which works out neatly at £1 per pipe.*

LEFT *A feature of the interior is the interplay between delicate decoration and broad mass – here is the metal tracery on the organ.*

OPPOSITE *Such a vast circus space encourages the thrill of blood sports – boxing may be ruled by Queensberry, but in this space it can feel gladiatorial.*

THE PAINTED HALL

Sir christopher wren's Great Hall (the Painted Hall) at Greenwich is described by the eminent 20th-century historian Sir John Summerson as a room of 'immense dignity'. He says that the Hall's grandeur of scale and proportion is underlined by James Thornhill's elaborate paintings – 'a triumph of richly coloured allegorical Baroque wall decoration'.

Likewise it has been said that the painting is so artful that Thornhill's decoration appears to open the ceilings to heaven. The religious themes are supplemented with depictions of maritime affairs (demanded by the patrons).

The Hall was originally intended as Greenwich Hospital's refectory, the upper section for officers and the lower for 'pensioners'. The interior, with its giant portico and central domed hall, flanked by staircases and an open courtyard, also resembles the layout of St Paul's – it has been described as Wren's rehearsal for St Paul's. For James Thornhill, its decoration was also a rehearsal for St Paul's because he was later chosen as the painter of the *Grisaille* panels inside the dome of the Cathedral.

Thornhill was England's best known mural painter and the only one who could challenge the many foreign decorative painters then working in England. His work is to be found also at Chatsworth, Hampton Court and at Blenheim. In 1718 he was appointed history painter to George I. Knighted in 1722 he was elected a Member of Parliament in the same year.

Thornhill charged for his work by the yard and originally asked for £5 a yard but was beaten down to £3 a yard for ceiling work and £1 a yard for wall work. In 1727 he thus received £6,685. Not a huge sum bearing in mind that Reubens received £4,000 a century earlier for his preliminary work on the ceiling of Inigo Jones's Banqueting House in Whitehall (see page 48).

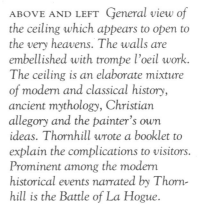

above and left *General view of the ceiling which appears to open to the very heavens. The walls are embellished with trompe l'oeil work. The ceiling is an elaborate mixture of modern and classical history, ancient mythology, Christian allegory and the painter's own ideas. Thornhill wrote a booklet to explain the complications to visitors. Prominent among the modern historical events narrated by Thornhill is the Battle of La Hogue.*

above *Detail of the west wall: George I surrounded by his family (on the steps are his grandchildren) receiving his sceptre from Peace, and watched over by Time with a horn of plenty tumbling with gold.*

opposite *Looking up into the dome which surmounts the entrance to the Great Hall – this dome has its partner in the King Charles block (the Painted Hall is in the King William block).*

SYON HOUSE

THE DUKE OF NORTHUMBERLAND commissioned Robert Adam to remodel the interior of Syon House (1762-69). The facing page shows the ante-room at Syon House. The transition as one walks from the white entrance hall into the ante-room's elaborate and colourful space is, as Adam intended, breathtaking. You can see the Entrance Hall on the left and perhaps you can get some sense of the passage from cool to rich, from whiteness to the bejewelled.

What sort of impression a contemporary visitor to the house was intended to receive is something of a mystery. The Entrance Hall is gracious but chilling, the ante-room is warm in its golds and greens but suffused – and with a hauteur that is intimidating. Very little in modern architecture prepares us for the scope and the scale of the grand interiors of the past. The 18th-century landed nobility was small, stable and, as well being rich, politically very powerful. Visitors would thus not be cowed, but they were surely meant to be impressed by the wealth and the sophistication of the new decoration. The 18th century was, after all, the century when English arts and crafts achieved its exquisite refinement before it was fundamentally altered by the Industrial Revolution. (Although refinement, however much it became built into the architecture, was not a natural characteristic of the age as this extract from the Duchess of Northumberland's diary reveals: '6 May 1760: Went home; voided a large stone. Tired to death. Went to ball; tired to death. A Bad Supper. Miss Townshend drunk.')

Scottish architect and designer Robert Adam (1728-92) worked in Rome for three years with his brother James, with whom, in Britain, he subsequently established an architectural practice. Robert Adam is famous for his domestic interiors and what is enjoyable about his work is the way he tempered the rational designs of Palladian classical style with vivacious decoration. It is a little like ruffling a well-dressed head of hair. You ought to be able to read a man's character in his art, and Adam has been described as an earnest, hardworking young man who liked his amusements. It shows. Adam designed right down to the merest detail – even the door fittings – everything was part of a unified scheme for him.

It is also intriguing to learn of the conflict between the popular tastes of the rich clients and the conservatism of some of Adam's rivals. Among the toughest of Robert Adam's rivals was Sir William Chambers (1723-96) – it seems he deplored Robert Adam's talent for decorative fancy and blocked Adam's membership of the Royal Academy. It would be interesting to learn whether the impetus for this was solely intellectual or whether Chambers was worried by the considerable commercial success of the Adams' firm. Adam was also responsible for redesigning Osterley Park House (see page 23).

FAR LEFT *The impressive black reclining statue in classical pose dominates the room.*

LEFT *Placed directly opposite the black figure for maximum symmetry and effect, this elegant figure is carved from dull white marble.*

OPPOSITE *This Neo-Classic 18th-century interior sums up all that was considered to be the epitome of good taste among the rich and powerful aristocrats of the period. We see here the height of this architectural style.*

HARRODS FOOD HALL

THE FOOD HALLS are the heart – or rather stomach – of Harrods, perhaps the most famous store in the world. The store rambles vastly from department to department but the Edwardian Food Halls have a coherence of purpose and identity and they celebrate food as entertainment, pageant and ceremony – it is a brilliant example of packaging. They have been extensively cleaned and restored in recent times.

Among the striking decorative features in the Food Hall is the tiled scene on the walls called *Scenes from the Hunt* by W. J. Neatby – done by Doulton's in 1902. Of course, one's own imagination can be overfed, but the displays and the decorations remind one of a wide variety of art – ranging from the bright, glazed salad colours of the della Robbias of sunny Italy, to the darker, more intense still-life paintings of the Netherlands. The Dutch, in their paintings, were masters and mistresses (some of the best 17th-century still-life painters were women) of celebrating food and exploiting the idea of the cornucopia. The Food Halls are in the centre of the store and there are no windows out into the world; it is like being in a great pantry, or a bizarre theatre. To that extent it is interesting that Francis Bacon, painter of tortured, meaty men, has been glimpsed here, gazing at the butchered meat.

Harrods does millions of pounds worth of trade a year in these halls alone. A large part of the food department, the grocery section, is designed as a superior supermarket. Food is a competitive business but the skill of the marketing is such that great attention has been paid to such details as nomenclature – the supermarket of groceries is actually called *The Pantry*. All in all it provides a peculiar 'peasant' decor for urban sophisticates.

Naturally, because Harrods is a store of great scale, massive pretension and shrewd commercial acumen, things like statistics matter a lot. In the official Harrods history reference is made, for example, to the 252 different kinds of bread on show, and how once it had a cake weighing one and a half hundredweight, which depicted outlandish scenes such as a family Christmas. Some of the fish sold by Harrods have been amongst the largest caught in Europe, and the store once sold a huge bottle of port called a Nebuchadnezzar - it was the equivalent of 48 ordinary sized bottles of port. One little-known strange drink sold by Harrods is called 'mezcal tequila', described as an amber tequila-like liquid in which floats a small worm. This is a delicacy.

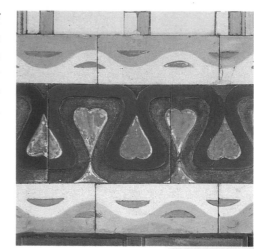

OPPOSITE *The Food Halls (built in 1901-3) are a triumph – it is the delicacy of the detailing that is admirable.*

ABOVE *Loosely-painted tiles create a snaking effect and are a great pleasure: would a modern decorator have such panache?*

ABOVE *Marble – for richness, reassurance and hygiene.*

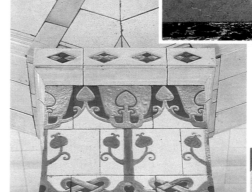

ABOVE AND RIGHT *Tiles that suggest echoes of Italy. Would a modern manager commission such boldness of detail?*

THE DORCHESTER

IN THE HEART OF MAYFAIR lies the Dorchester: one of the world's great hotels. It declares luxury, style, money and grace but it does it with finesse, not vulgarity. It is not an old hotel and indeed grew, or rather sprang up, at the beginning of the 1930s, the decade of the cocktail.

The building, designed by William Curtis Green, a Royal Academician, began in September 1930 and opened to the public eight months later. In fact the foundation plans were by the engineer Sir Owen Williams (see page 58) but there had been a row between him and McAlpine and Sons, then joint owners of the hotel with the Gordon group.

The Dorchester's interior is particularly associated with the designer Oliver Messel (1904-1978) whose mother, Maud, was the daughter of Linley Sambourne (see page 71). Messel studied at the Slade (one of his contemporaries was the artist Rex Whistler). Messel's early professional work was for Diaghilev, the great choreographer, and from this beginning he went on to do a number of stage sets. As his career matured he worked for Covent Garden and the Metropolitan Opera House in New York.

In 1953 Messel designed the luxury suite on the seventh floor of the Dorchester and the Penthouse suite; in 1955 he designed the Pavilion Room. He was a close friend of Noel Coward and Coward stayed at the Dorchester from time to time. One can hear the exaggeratedly crisp *hauteur* of Coward's voice in one of his diary entries which reads: 'I am home in England again installed in the somewhat excessive *luxe* of the Oliver Messel Suite.'

The ambience of the bar, designed by Alberto Pinto, a Parisian interior decorator, is one of languor and its blue, white and cream decor and plump, snug leather seating are strongly suggestive of one of the pre-war luxury liners.

This bar, replacing the original one of the late 1930s, opened in 1981. During the rebuilding a 'time capsule' was discovered; it had been left by the then head barman, Harry Craddock and gave recipes for five cocktails as well as phials with samples.

The Dorchester was bought by the Sultan of Brunei, and closed for one year from Christmas 1988 (not long after these photographs were taken) for an extensive refurbishment to maintain the hotel's world class reputation. In Spring 1990 patrons will, once more, be able to sample cocktails in the Dorchester and much, much more besides.

TOP *The Promenade, with an Italian marble floor, 18th-century Chinese tapestries, and a suspended coffered ceiling.*

ABOVE *A table setting in the Penthouse Suite.*

OPPOSITE *The Alberto Pinto bar. The French tiles painted with exotic birds are by the La Morinerie company. The walls are panelled with limed oak.*

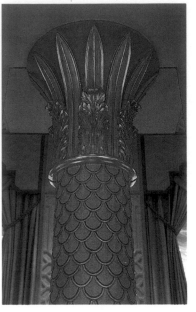

ABOVE One of the fibrous plaster columns in the Terrace Restaurant. The fish scale pattern is embellished with 24-carat gold leaf.

LEFT The Terrace Restaurant, designed by Alberto Pinto. The style is described as Rococo Regency with the dominant colours being coral pink, yellow and cream. The pink and cream damask linen is from Ireland and the silk curtains come from France. The tables are set for dinner.

LLOYD'S OF LONDON

PEOPLE ARE EXTRAORDINARY. On the one hand the executives of Lloyd's of London commissioned Richard Rogers, one of Europe's most radical architects, to design their new headquarters. On the other hand, the members of the Lloyd's Council meet in a Robert Adam interior. The Adam interior, designed for Bowood House in Wiltshire, was rebuilt and housed high up in the carapace of Rogers' steel and aluminium construction. When you look out of one of the Adam windows you look out into a Rogers corridor. Thus the Adam room is literally a stage set – and that is fascinating.

Lloyd's is very much a part of the 'real' world, part of the core of the world's most important, high-tech service industry – money. Moreover, Rogers' building is, externally, a striking metaphor for all that is modern. And yet the Council prefers to make up its mind in the graceful surroundings of the 18th century. Perhaps this is not a surprise. Men at the top have long preferred to make their decisions in domestic rather than office interiors. The rooms of top civil servants are more like the sitting rooms of their homes or the common rooms of their old colleges. And Adam's sense of the domestic is hardly suburban.

ABOVE *Detail of the units that house the lighting, air conditioning and fire extinguishing systems.*

LEFT *A detail of the Adam ceiling and wall decorations.*

FAR LEFT *The Robert Adam room where the Lloyd's Council meets – a unique combination of extremes. This perfectly reconstructed 18th-century interior is housed in the middle of one of the most unusual – and even outrageous – modern buildings in London today.*

Richard Rogers came to public attention when, with Renzo Piano, he designed the Pompidou Arts Centre in Paris. It seemed then, as it does now with the Lloyd's building, that Rogers' main ambition is to turn buildings inside out. Consequently, there is a lot to see on the outside of Lloyd's and the building is helped in its zinc-coloured and silvery metalness by the classical modern simplicity of neighbours like the Commercial Union building across the road. But inside, thanks to the 200-feet high atrium, there are also stunning views.

As a result of the specially designed windows the light on the ground floor is soothing and, on sunny days, it has a mellow quality as if it were being diffused through a clear sea. The glass of the windows sparkles – this is because of the pimples that were incorporated when the glass was rolled. As the Rogers' Partnership handbook on the building notes: 'During day-time the sparkle glass acts as a translucent wall of light, but at night the surface refracts artificial light back into the occupied space, creating a bright, animated effect, not unlike cut crystal.'

The photograph overleaf shows the view looking down into the atrium. The eye pivots on the Rostrum, the traditional meeting or focal point of Lloyd's which has been taken from the old Lloyd's headquarters. The Rostrum houses the famous Lutine bell which is rung to announce news of overdue vessels or when there is an event of special importance. Despite the sophistication of the electronic communications present in this building the members like to cling to the continuity of tradition.

ABOVE In this book the major disasters of each day are recorded. Beyond we can see the famous Lutine bell rung at events of especial importance.

LEFT The atrium is exciting; the galleries around the atrium can be brought into commission (or taken out of commission) as and when business expands. When not required the space can be let.

OPPOSITE The view down the central atrium of the huge Lloyd's building. At 200 feet it is probably the world's tallest 'room'. This is the Rostrum, the meeting place for the Lloyd's members. Glass and tubular pillars create a surreal space-age environment that is full of light and space. The light has a curiously diffused and sparkling effect, which is due to the special way in which the glass was manufactured.

WESTMINSTER ABBEY

The NAVE OF WESTMINSTER ABBEY is one of the glories of English architecture, an interior of drama, mystery and audacity, although now often too much crowded by an unending clutter of loud tourists and visitors.

The design of Westminster is in part attributed to a master mason named Henry Yevele, but how much is him and how much is the design of the clerics who employed him is not known. However, Yevele was in charge of the rebuilding of the nave to the design as we see it today and, in fact, the style in which he designed was 'old-fashioned'. For in 1376 the current fashion was the 'Decorated' style, but Yevele rebuilt in the style established 100 years earlier during Henry III's reign.

This Medieval building today may fit our conception of a Medieval atmosphere but we are misled. When the Abbey was complete, the interior was limewashed and the carvings were either painted bright colours or gilded. Colours celebrated both God and Man, and the intensity of colour, so much taken for granted these days, was a rare experience then. Moreover, there was a delicate screen across the chancel (not the Victorian screen and organ sitting there today) and the place was of course empty of the many monuments that now embellish it.

The great architectural historian Nikolaus Pevsner says that what distinguishes the interior of Westminster Abbey from the interior of other English Medieval churches is its height in relation to its width. As such its proportions are comparable to the French cathedrals of Reims and Amiens. Westminster Abbey presents a theatrical compression of the imagination into a single-minded concentration upon the mystery of God.

LEFT *Interior of the nave, Westminster Abbey (1376–1517), looking east towards the chancel. The screen is early 19th-century. The architect, Henry Yevele (or his employer, the Abbot Litlyngton) were at work on the nave in the late 14th century, continuing the work begun in the 13th.*

RIGHT *The ceiling at the crossing with the transepts – here we see the lantern which, says the historian Pevsner, looks highly temporary and unfinished. This is a glorious piece of engineering.*

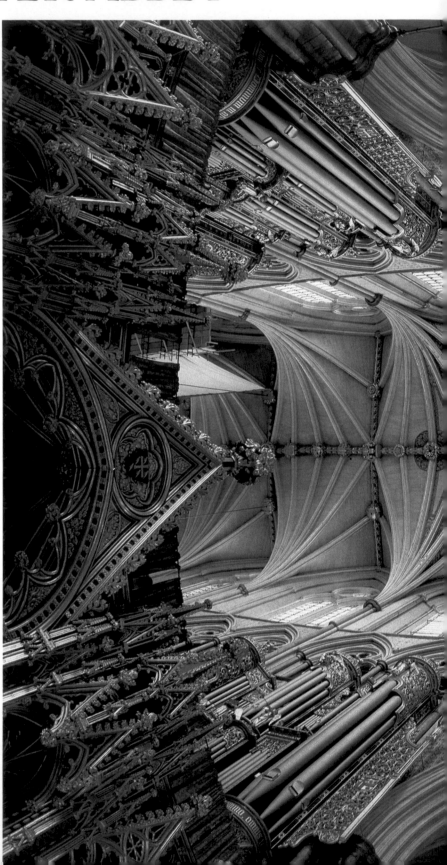

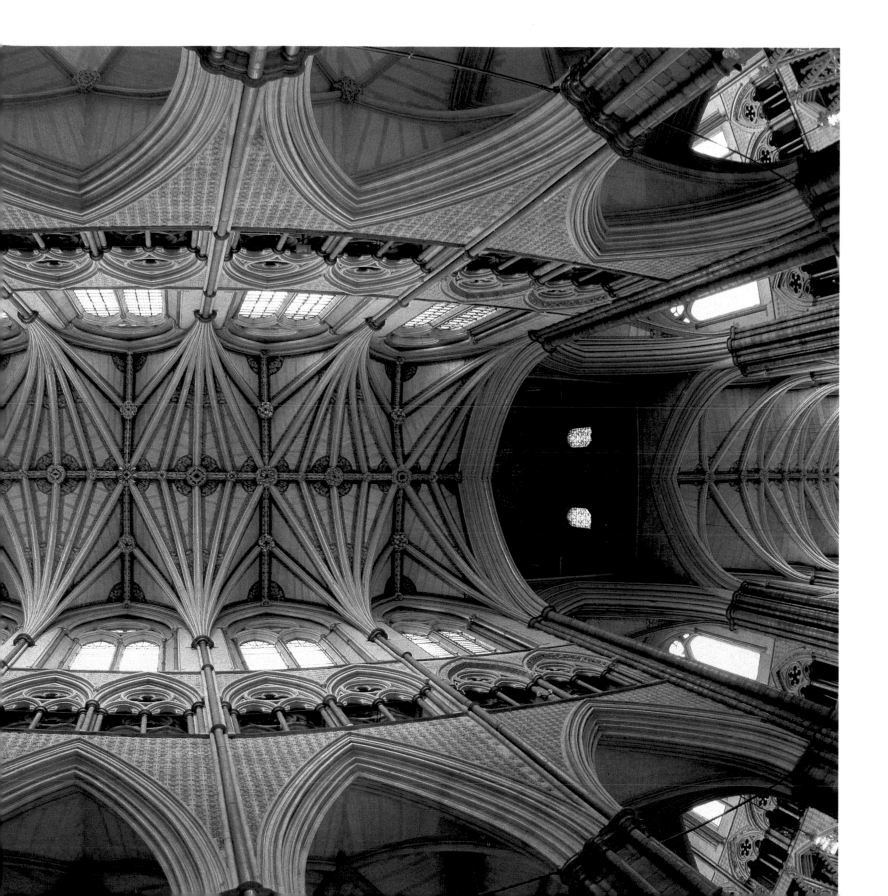

REGENT'S PARK MOSQUE

PERHAPS A FORGOTTEN but nevertheless significant fact about the British Empire is that it was an Empire with more Muslim than Christian inhabitants. Understandably, leading Muslims felt that a mosque should be built in London.

The major impetus for this building was political expediency: in early 1940 the Chairman of the British Council persuaded Prime Minister Neville Chamberlain that a place of worship in the Empire's Capital was only just; moreover, although the Muslims were allies they were feeling somewhat lukewarm towards Britian. It was felt they might be more positive if a gesture of recognition was made. Money was set aside and a trust formed, but it was not until 1970 and a new trust, together with representations from Saudi Arabia, Pakistan, the Lebanon and Kuwait, that the building started. An international competition was organised and the winner was Sir Fredrick Gibberd, architect of the innovative Catholic Cathedral in Liverpool. The building was begun in 1974, although when construction began Gibberd's design was modified to make it more palatable to Muslim taste.

The site is also home to the Islamic Cultural Centre, whose extensive activities are educational, cultural and religious. A lot of the work is directed towards young people but the Centre is also open to the public and is used by many professional groups, including doctors, engineers and lawyers.

The building is decorated with woven carpet, chandeliers, mosaics and tiles. But the architectural detailing is pared down, partly because a sense of elaboration is given by the repetition of form. A characteristic of the building is its spaciousness – in the congregational prayer hall there are just four columns, each with a mushroom-shaped head, supporting the roof slabs.

The hall and dome present a fabulous interior, not through richness of decoration but because of the rhythm of volumes and flat patterns – this is assisted by the patterned floor of the hall and the thin, screen-like delicacy of the ladies' prayer area.

ABOVE *Detail of the frieze which forms a decorative horizon to the dome.*

LEFT *The mihrab, or pulpit, on the ground floor.*

OPPOSITE *The main congregational prayer hall. The space arches over those praying and creates a sense of theatre and awe. The advantage of a non-figurative, rhythmic decorative art is that the interior is contemplative; being abstract, the mind is free to concentrate on the universal rather than the particular. Modernist architecture we see was not the first to free itself from the distractions of the figurative.*

DURBAR COURT, FOREIGN OFFICE

DURBAR COURT IS PART of the Foreign Office in King Charles Street. It was the jewel of the old India Office when it opened in 1867 hosting a State Ball for the Sultan of Turkey. A century later, in the age of wiping all slates clean, Durbar Court was earmarked for demolition. The hammer may have been withheld, but the building was allowed to fall apart – its once grand role stripped bare to simply one of storage, and therefore without a maintenance budget. Pigeon droppings corroded some of the stonework, while the terracotta detailing and modelling were shattered and the tops of the pillars eroded. The mosaic and tiling were damaged over the years and the court itself subsided by four inches.

The decision to refurbish the building was prompted partly by a change in opinion – the 1980s has a taste for Victorian elaborations – and partly because the Foreign Office needed more office space. The refurbishment has been well done but with a judicious eye on costs. For example, the gorgeous but damaged mosaic frieze has been patched up with painted plaster – can we tell the difference? Perhaps time will tell.

The architect of the main office had been George Gilbert Scott, but he had a huge and public row with the Prime Minister, Lord Palmerston. Scott, who also designed St Pancras Hotel (see page 80), was a master of the Gothic style. Palmerston wanted a more classical design. In the event, and although Scott clung like fury to the overall contract, Durbar Court was created by Matthew Digby Wyatt (who also wrought the architectural trimmings on Brunel's Paddington Station).

Durbar Court is hard to classify – it is very rich in its surface embellishments but the decoration is framed by granite and sandstone. The plain, round arches of the colonnades are more reminiscent of Romanesque than Gothic. The bizarre optical effects of the Dutch graphic artist Escher spring to mind, because as you follow the arches round, your eye comes back to where you started and yet you feel as though you have tracked up and down and around all the levels. Nothing is over-egged. The regiment of portrait busts are framed in a classical manner, and this strong nod towards imperialism is more in keeping with the Headquarters of Empire. Victorian Gothic is generally just that shade too bourgeois to be convincingly imperial (although it is fine for railway stations). The court was intended to be open to the air but was given a steel and glass roof which has protected it from bad weather over the years.

ABOVE *The mosaic frieze is generally seen at some distance; you are unlikely to detect the restoration in painted plaster. The delicacy of the ceiling decoration recalls India and Persia – echoes consistent with the 18th-century belief that Gothic had its roots in India and was imported to Western Europe via Persia.*

LEFT AND BELOW LEFT *Among the pleasures neglected by late 20th-century architects is the drama of architectural perspectives – and the combination here of granite and sandstone creates particularly gracious vistas.*

OPPOSITE *The angularity of the iron and glass roof creates a puritanical foil to the building although the restraint of the colonnades ensures the court is not over-egged in its impact.*

THE BANQUETING HOUSE

THE BANQUETING HOUSE, Whitehall was designed by Inigo Jones and is considered his greatest achievement. Its building began in 1619 and was completed four years later. The interior space is both impressive and dramatic – the great panels of the ceiling hold paintings by Sir Peter Paul Rubens. Yet the interior feels empty because it was designed as a stage, a setting for masques and grand receptions. Accordingly the interior was (and still is) completed by the nature of the dressings used for specific occasions.

Inigo Jones had an extraordinary career and is described as brilliant and arrogant. He came from a poor family but went to Italy, presumably in the retinue of a nobleman, where he saw and was excited by the masques which the Medici family of Florence staged. Indeed it was as a producer of masques that he first made his reputation. On his return to England Inigo Jones secured various jobs and eventually he became the Surveyor of the King's Works. His impact on London was immense – he introduced formal town planning to the city, with the first London 'square' at Covent Garden.

The interior of the Banqueting House is 110 feet long, 55 feet wide and 55 feet high. It is divided into two storeys by a balustraded gallery. The whole is divided into seven 15-foot bays by pilasters; these are Ionic in style below the gallery and Corinthian above it. It is conceived internally as a basilica without aisles. The superimposed columns support a flat beamed ceiling.

The space is dominated however by the rampant, billowing swollen paintings high above on the ceiling. The huge output, let alone quality, of the painter Sir Peter Paul Rubens (1577-1640) is a source of amazement. Rubens studied the paintings of Titian and Veronese, and art historians say the influence of both is visible in the work in the Banqueting House.

The paintings are heroic and celebrate the sagacity of James I of England (and King of Scotland as James VI) – the self-styled 'King of Great Britain'. The order of the paintings has been changed over the years, but the present configuration, positioned in 1972, is thought to be how Charles 1 and Rubens envisaged them on their installation in 1635. What Charles did not envisage at the time was that almost 15 years later he would walk through the Banqueting House for the last time. On January 30th 1649 he made his way out on to the scaffold through one of the windows and was beheaded.

ABOVE *The ceiling of the Banqueting House was painted by Sir Peter Paul Rubens. The panel on the left, which is above the entrance, depicts the union of England and Scotland with, at the top, Hercules representing Strength and Minerva representing Wisdom. The middle panel is the* Apotheosis of James I. *This shows the monarch, one foot on an eagle and the other on the imperial globe. He is about to be raised to heaven – on his right are two female figures, one symbolising Religion and the other Scriptural Truth. The earthly symbols of royal power – the crown and orb – are taken away by cherubs. The panel on the right, above the throne, is* The Benefits of James's I Government *with, at the top, Royal Bounty and below Wise Government.*

OPPOSITE *The impressive interior flanked by 14 Corinthian-style pilasters above the gallery, and Ionic-style below. Even with Rubens' fine ceiling paintings, the interior feels 'bare' – and such was the architect's intention because the grand room was meant to complement whatever occasions graced the hall, be it masque or feast, to pay tribute to the monarch.*

THE HOUSE OF LORDS

THE HOUSE OF LORDS is part of a collection of buildings known as the Palace of Westminster. As the seat of British Government it has survived both verbal and physical attacks. Although Guy Fawkes did not achieve his aim, a fire did destroy much of it in 1834, as did a Second World War bombing raid just over a century later.

The House of Lords, the upper chamber of the Palace of Westminster, was opened in 1847. The architect of the Houses of Parliament was Sir Charles Barry (with his son taking over after his death); but the architect and designer Augustus Pugin made a considerable contribution with all the Gothic detailing. Pugin was the architect of the Gothic Revival, perhaps the most potent of 19th-century architectural styles.

How one responds to Victorian Gothic is obviously a matter of taste: the fashion for deriding it as mere pastiche (which in the hands of Pugin it clearly is not) has now passed. However, as you look at the interiors of the Palace of Westminster, especially those of the House of Lords, you are struck by the self-image – a portentous self-image – that the Government and the 'ruling class' had (and continues to have) of itself.

The style is formal, very elaborate and rather heavy. It seems that there are two kinds of 'English style' – a light, pastoral one, and a heavy, somnolent and dark fuggish one. Moreover, impressive and fascinating though this work is, the obsessive piling-in of detail and ornament seems to predict the madness which later afflicted Pugin.

In the House of Lords we see the ornateness and heaviness of an invented tradition, a building that pretends to look older than it is. A beguiling interior, it has the sense of appropriateness for courtly, mannered debate. The focal point of the chamber is the throne for the Monarch – she (or he) is not permitted into the House of Commons.

Cardinal Newman said, 'Mr Pugin is a man of genius . . . His zeal, his minute diligence, his resources, his invention, his imagination, his sagacity in research, are all of the highest order. But he has the great fault of a man of genius, as well as the merit. He is intolerant and . . . sees nothing good in any school of Christian art except that of which he is himself so great an ornament.' Thank God for the man's faults, they gave him the obsessive direction he needed to make the fine detailing we see here.

ABOVE *Chamber of the House of Lords looking towards the royal throne. Between the decorated arches behind the throne are statues of the barons who backed the* Magna Carta.

LEFT *The Royal Robing Room. This is the room in which the reigning monarch puts on the Parliamentary Robes and the Imperial Crown for the State Opening of Parliament. On the left of the portrait of Queen Victoria can be seen one of the frescoes by William Dyce depicting scenes from Arthurian legend. Dyce was commissioned to do these as a result of a competition instigated by Prince Albert, who made sure that the whole of the Palace of Westminster was furnished with the arts, and whose portrait can be seen on the right of the throne.*

OPPOSITE *The Royal Gallery: a quintessential interior of England – gold, red and lit with the mellowness of stained glass. The 45-foot fresco is one of a pair painted by Daniel Maclise, and is entitled* The Death of Nelson.

THE OLD BAILEY

THE OLD BAILEY or, to give it the proper title of The Central Criminal Court, stands on the site of Newgate Prison, infamous since the 11th century as a place of incarceration and execution.

The first Old Bailey opened in 1539; it was replaced in 1774 but this was itself demolished with Newgate Prison in 1902 to make way for the third and present building, opened in 1907 by Edward VII. The more modern extensions south and east were added in 1972.

The Old Bailey is the property of the Corporation of London and still honours many of the old traditions. For example, four times each year the Lord Mayor as the City's Chief Justice formally visits in state to open the Session. Poesies are carried on these occasions; a reminder of 1750 when the Lord Mayor and four members of the bench died from gaol fever, or typhus. The poesies were believed to ward off the disease.

The current building opened in 1907 and was designed by E.W. Mountford. It is a piece of Edwardian Baroque worked out through the language of Christopher Wren, and embel-lished with tricks and fancies developed through the Arts and Crafts movement. It was a public style, a civic style, and it expressed confidence and commitment to public values. It flourished in the great provincial cities of Liverpool, Manchester and Glasgow.

The Old Bailey was influenced both inside and externally by St Paul's. Clad in Portland stone like the cathedral, it is topped with a copper dome on which the statue by Pomeroy, the figure of Justice, stands – one of the most famous public images in the Western world. Cast in bronze and covered in gold leaf, she bears the scales of justice and sword of retribution.

The interior is stunning: the floors are of Sicilian marble with strips of Belgian black, Swedish green and panels of Siena marble. The walls are lined with verderasse and Hopton wood; the archways are of white Ancaster stone and the 16-foot columns are of cipollino and verde antico. The grandeur and symbolism of the Grand Hall is an expression of great confidence, strength and dignity. It provides a sense of occasion, history, continuity and communality.

FAR LEFT *The Grand Hall looking south towards No 1 Court and the New Building. The figures are of Sir Thomas Gresham and Charles I by John Bushnell from the second Royal Exchange of 1671. The painting, by Moira in 1906, depicts figures representative of city life paying homage to Justice on the steps of St Paul's.*

LEFT *The small window shows the coats of arms of the more notable Recorders of London. The larger window depicts the arms of the City of London, Edward II and Middlesex, surrounded by the coats of arms of counties over which the courts have jurisdiction.*

ABOVE *The dome viewed from below, damaged by enemy action in 1941 but restored by Moira with four paintings celebrating Art, Truth, Labour and Learning with, between them, the four swords and the Mace of the City.*

RIGHT *The statue of Elizabeth Fry by Alfred Drury stands in the Old Bailey in recognition of her work as a prison reformer: she first visited the old Newgate Prison in 1813 and the conditions there so appalled her that her life was devoted to reform.*

OVERLEAF *The Grand Hall looking north to the area destroyed by the 1941 bomb but restored by Moira in 1954. The sculpted figures in relief below the dome are by Pomeroy, and depict Justice, Mercy, Charity and Temperence. The painting reflects arts, learning and industry – Sir Edmund Hillary and Everest are shown in the right-hand corner. The 1671 statue is of Charles II.*

KEY TO EXTERIORS

THE BRITISH MUSEUM
Great Russell Street
Bloomsbury WC1

NATIONAL WESTMINSTER BANK
Threadneedle Street
The City EC2

THE GUILDHALL
Basinghall Street
The City EC2

THE GRANADA BINGO HALL
Mitcham Road
Tooting SW17

APSLEY HOUSE
Hyde Park Corner
Knightsbridge W1

LANCASTER HOUSE
Stable Yard
St James's SW1

OSTERLEY PARK HOUSE
Heston
Isleworth W7

THE ROYAL OPERA HOUSE
Bow Street
Covent Garden WC2

THE ROYAL ALBERT HALL
Kensington Gore
Knightsbridge SW7

THE PAINTED HALL
Royal Naval College
Greenwich SE10

SYON HOUSE
London Road
Brentford TW8

HARRODS FOOD HALL
Brompton Road
Knightsbridge SW1

THE DORCHESTER
Park Lane
Mayfair W1

LLOYD'S OF LONDON
Lime Street
The City EC3

WESTMINSTER ABBEY
Broad Sanctuary
Westminster SW1

LONDON CENTRAL MOSQUE
Park Road
Regent's Park NW8

THE FOREIGN OFFICE
Whitehall
St James's SW1

THE BANQUETING HOUSE
Whitehall
St James's SW1

THE HOUSE OF LORDS
Parliament Square
Westminster SW1

THE OLD BAILEY
Strand
Holborn EC4

CHAPTER TWO

Moments Preserved

Few of us would remain unmoved or unreflective when confronted with some aspect of our childhood – chancing upon a toy or a photographic album perhaps. Even more compelling is the desire to touch something that existed well before our own birth.

It is fashionable in some intellectual circles and among 'raze-to-the-ground' property developers to mock people's affections for the past. *Nostalgia* is regarded as weakness, and the nostalgia or heritage industry is derided as a sign of the country's underlying decline, and as an inability to cope with the present.

Stuff and nonsense. There is no evidence to suggest that a wish to stay connected to the past is a denial of the present or a fear of the future. Indeed, the country has scarcely embraced the future with so much enthusiasm as it has in the late 20th century. But amid change we want to hold on to fragments of the past and maintain continuity, families try to do it all the time. The moments preserved here are Everyman's.

OPPOSITE: *The Prince Henry Room, at No 17 Fleet Street in the half-timbered building above the gateway to the Inner Temple. It is a masculine, ponderous room, suitable for the expensive musings of lawyers; a true interior expression of Dickens' Jarndyce and Jarndyce.*

ABOVE: *A scene from Dennis Severs' House (see page 98). Spitalfields, where this house is located, was a centre for weaving and also an area favoured by immigrants – first the French, then the Jews and today the Asians (and in particular, Bengalis). This house is a living 'museum' testifying to 200 years of history.*

THE EXPRESS BUILDING

Sir Owen Williams, an eminent civil engineer, designed the Express newspaper building which opened in 1931. It was an advanced building for the period being a simple black glass block with very little exterior decoration. It was a dramatic addition to Fleet Street, but the drama intensifies as soon as you enter the foyer. The black chic austerity outside does not prepare you for the glizty, electric mother-of-pearl decor inside – it is another example of the drama of passage that architects and interior designers can prepare for us. Here, it is like going inside a chocolate box.

Sir Nikolaus Pevsner, perhaps our best loved arbiter of architectural taste (after Betjeman) tolerates the exterior but loathes the interior – he could not stand the lumpen expressionism in the murals and the exaggerated lines of the zig-zag detailing. The foyer, designed by Robert Atkinson, was completed in 1932.

The style is Art Deco, a style largely put together by interior decorators after the First World War. Apparently it was the style of the new rich – an assertion of 'If you've got it, flaunt it.'

The variety of visual references includes traces of Gothic in the ceiling and hints of Egypt in the figures. It has been suggested that the central approach to the main staircase is in the spirit of the entrance to Cleopatra's tomb. The interior is reminiscent, in fact, of a cinema. Cinema architecture of the period was rampant in its eclecticism and cinemas laid down the popular bench mark for luxury.

The zig-zag, the geometric flowers, the scallop shapes and an almost wanton zeal in the use of electric lighting is typical of the style. But unlike so many passing fashions in which the trumpery is thin and poorly made, a lot of Art Deco artefacts and decoration were made from good materials and finished to a high standard of workmanship. This is true here.

One of the recurrent Art Deco motifs is that of the snake – it is here in the foyer – and one wonders why. Is it because it adds a sense of the exotic and provides allusions to sex, temptation and devilry? Exotic and sexual innuendo are often an important element in kitsch – and kitsch provides the brio in Art Deco.

ABOVE *This detail is of one of the chromium twisted snakes which act as handrails up to the main staircase.*

RIGHT *This detail from one of the two Aumantier raised metal murals represents the extensive reaches of the Empire, its trade and its communications.*

FAR RIGHT *The tiered ceiling is a typical Art Deco device that sustains the rhythm of ascent, pulling the eye to sky.*

OPPOSITE *This is Ronald Atkinson and Eric Aumantier's foyer with its extensive use of monometal (a forerunner of aluminium). The high-quality craftsmanship is a feature of Art Deco that has not been sustained in the quasi-Art Deco decoration which has crept into 'post-modernism'. The startling, elongated boss, where the ribs of the fan vault meet, has been artfully lit to maximise the effectiveness of the ceiling's form.*

THE EEL AND PIE SHOP

LIKE FISH AND CHIPS the eel and pie is a working class dish (as indeed, were oysters) – nourishing, cheap and, even more so than fish and chips, very old-fashioned to modern eyes and taste.

One of the oddities of modern 'convenience' food is its lack of correspondence with the living thing it was made from. This is especially true of the post-war American-style fast food franchises. Burgers, chicken sticks and the like have no resemblance to flesh or fowl. But the jellied eel – that is quite different and, perhaps, declares its pedigree just too closely for modern sensibilities. For some of us the eel is off-putting – the quick, slippery and nervy creature is never *quite* dead enough. And at F. Cooke's a tankful of live eels is kept ready at the back.

The family firm running this shop has been going for more than a century since 1862, and the shop's 1910 tiled and decorated interior provides a direct connection between us, the common people of now, with them, the common people of Dickens' era. And this makes the shop special because most of the things that become preserved or which manage to continue functioning in the late 20th century celebrate the grandeur of Church, State or Commerce. And so, whilst the Harrods Food Hall (see page 34) is a lovely place it is hardly a conduit of historical connection to the ordinary man or woman. It is the small change of ordinary life in the past which is intriguing as well as the grander slams of nobility.

Not that one should romanticise London's East End which was in many respects vile. But nor should we overlook its architectural treats. This restaurant would have been 'state of the art' when it opened – all those tiles, although pretty, are also hygienic. It was in the latter half of the 19th century that the foundations of public health legislation, standards of hygiene and the like were established. Moreover this eel and pie shop is kitted out to the allegedly 20th-century philosophy of 'form follows function'. Except that here the form and the function are married together with decorative flair. And, though remarking earlier that the food was cheap and nourishing, there is, nevertheless, nothing down-at-heel about this shop – it has some style, it would have been almost *posh*.

The shop still serves a working constituency and although it is possible that it will become cocooned as a place for visitors, for the moment it does do more than feed the sentiments of backward-lookingness.

ABOVE *Charming and individual pieces of artisan signage such as this were commonplace in the 19th century; today the skill and confidence of artisan craftsmen has been swamped by professional 'designers'.*

ABOVE *Very finely drawn hands and heads are characteristic of most Victorian decorative glass: it is the Dickensian fascination with facts again.*

LEFT *Clearly the pace of change was slower – no franchisee today would commit his or her menu to such permanence.*

ABOVE *In modern cafés things are either in cupboards or left in heaps, but not here – everything is artfully crafted into a display.*

LEFT *This interior was modern in its time – and it is still efficient: the tile and marble surfaces are easy to keep clean; the mirrors add to the general brightness, a great bonus in the gloom of polluted late Victorian London. The general standard of repair is very high and the place is softened with little domestic touches such as house plants.*

THE WHITEHALL THEATRE

THE WHITEHALL THEATRE like Whitehall in general is famous for its farces. Whether it was Members of Parliament losing their trousers on a train or Brain Rix dropping them nightly in the theatre throughout the 1950s and 1960s – for 24 years Whitehall staged farces.

Brian Rix, who used to manage the Whitehall Theatre and act in the plays, is still regarded as the man of farces. These days he also pursues charitable works and campaigns for better treatment and equitable legislation on behalf of the mentally handicapped. Moreover, the man who masterminded many a plot featuring bare male legs in shirt tails and socks, is a Knight – Sir Brian. Well, as they might say on the boards, 'Once a Knight, always a Knight and twice a Knight, you're doing all right!'.

The Whitehall opened in 1930 and its exterior reflects the hard, European-influenced *modernism* that was then fashionable – you can see the style cropping up in Southern England seaside resorts as well as in more portentous buildings such as the Senate House of the University of London (see page 229).

Whitehall was commissioned by a playwright called Walter Hackett. He wrote the first season of plays, his wife Marion Lorne acted in them, and the theatre prospered. The first play was Hackett's 'The Way To Treat A Woman'.

During the War the theatre showed the West End's first stripper – Phyllis Dixey. Apparently she kept up a funny banter with the audience as she unpeeled before them. Phyllis Dixey was astute, her revue did well and in 1944 she bought the lease of the theatre. After the immensely successful farces of the next 20 years or so Paul Raymond took over the theatre and staged 'Pyjama Tops'. But in 1983 he rather took the theatre world by surprise when he stopped putting on live entertainment and turned the theatre into a First and Second World War museum. It was not much liked by historians or design critics.

Raymond sold the theatre and today the theatre presents lively comedy both contemporary and period – there was John Well's sharpish fun in 'Anyone For Denis' (Thatcher) and there has been 'When We Were Married' by J.B. Priestley.

By current fashionable standards in theatre design, in which decoration is restricted to the neo-Stalinist textures of down lighting on bare shuttered concrete surfaces, the Whitehall interior appears quite elaborate in its mixture of art nouveau and art deco ornament. It is a reminder that, for Londoners, 'going up West' was once an event, a real treat.

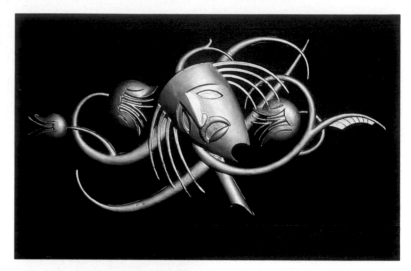

ABOVE *The mask of tragedy. The tendril decoration (LEFT) is painted to give a trompe l'oeil effect; the attenuated brittle-thin ornamentation is repeated on the proscenium arch. The painted murals have gentle nature as their content but the fragmentary composition derives from cubism.*

LEFT *The lovely trumpet-tongued mural recreates the sounds of jazz and big bands and the rich noise that comes out of wooden-cased valve radio sets.*

OPPOSITE *The central feature in the auditorium space is an octagonal ceiling design. The octagon is a typical 1930s shape.*

WYNDHAM'S THEATRE

CHARLES WYNDHAM'S THEATRE in Charing Cross Road opened in November 1899 in the presence of the Prince of Wales (who was, reportedly, delighted with the architecture). Indeed the theatre was regarded as the height of sophistication. It was designed by W. G. R. Sprague.

Charles Wyndham had an interesting life – he served as a surgeon in the Confederate army during the American Civil War, was an amateur actor for a while and then made his professional debut at the Royalty Theatre in London in 1862. Wyndham was able to build his theatre through the support of the Marquis of Salisbury. Salisbury was, at this point, Prime Minister. He owned the land on which the theatre stands, and he refused to allow any theatre to be built on it unless it was called Charles Wyndham's, as Wyndham was his favourite actor. Wyndham starred in the theatre's opening play 'David Garrick', written by T. W. Robertson.

In 1910 Charles Wyndham's acting company was joined by Gerald Du Maurier, the famous actor; his daughter Daphne Du Maurier, the writer and playwright, saw her play 'The Years Between' staged at Wyndham's in 1931.

The theatre's roll of honour of famous premières includes Sandy Wilson's 'The Boyfriend' and David Essex in 'Godspell'. A number of other important and adventurous plays have been staged here including Shelagh Delaney's 'A Taste of Honey' and the acerbic and wittily subversive anti-war musical 'Oh What A Lovely War' staged by the Joan Littlewood Theatre Workshop.

It was a great place for posing – a place to see and be seen in. Today its interior still seems sumptuous because modern times (being what they are), modern style (being what it is) and modern thrift have all combined to give us plain, shuttered concrete theatres. These modern interiors function beautifully, and plain concrete suits the tendentious gloom of Pinter and Hare, but it hardly feels like a celebratory night out. They don't write plays like they used to, nor decorate theatres.

Today Wyndham's is one of six West End theatres owned by Maybox and in 1988 it was declared by Lord Litchfield, the photographer, to be one of the best theatres in the world. Of course, even the best in the world has had its rough times architecturally speaking and someone in the 1960s (what *was* it about the 60s?) thought it would be a wacky idea to paint the interior in brown and margarine-coloured paint. Thankfully in 1972 the theatre was restored to its original blue and cream splendour.

ABOVE *The angels above the front of the stage are holding portraits of Richard Sheridan and Oliver Goldsmith.*

RIGHT *One of the delights of the older theatre is the tier upon elaborate tier of decoration – escalating like one's expectations as the time approaches for the curtain to rise.*

OPPOSITE *The lavish detailing of the theatre roof (above) extends over the audience like an exotic sky. And the stage curtains (below) are an exact copy of the original – the design is deliberately lopsided.*

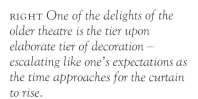

THE HOP EXCHANGE

THE HOP EXCHANGE, which occupies an acre of ground near London Bridge, was designed by R. H. Moore and opened for business in 1867. Fortunately most of the building (apart from part of the west wing) survived the Blitz and the years of post-War demolition although it was partly destroyed in 1918 by fire. Hops are dried ripe flowers of the hop plant which are used in brewing beer to provide the bitter taste. Unsurprisingly, this area was once densely populated with independent breweries most of which have now closed or long been sunk down the throats of one of the big corporate beer manufacturers.

The hops came in the main from Kent, the centre of hop growing, and every harvest time thousands of Londoners would 'holiday' by becoming hop pickers, earning money and escaping into the fresh air at one and the same time. The hops were taken from Kent to London by rail. The 19th century, greatly assisted by the railways and (later) the invention of the telegraph, saw the rapid centralisation of trade and commerce pushing London into its current egregiousness and distorting forever the fabric of the south-east of England. The 'London effect' has gradually nibbled away at the beauty and isolation of what was once the 'garden of England'. The Channel Tunnel and its rail and road lines will further exacerbate the urbanisation.

The importance of the Hop Exchange building rests in its interior elegance, with the cast iron structure supporting the galleries and the beautifully composed windows and doorways leading to the individual offices. The central area is the former exchange space and it has a glass roof. Its upgrading into modern offices has been a commercial success due to the demand for 'older buildings with character' and by its proximity to London Bridge railway station, although the restoration was undertaken by Peer Group plc in the early 1980s before the rent levels had accelerated.

BELOW *Details of the iron balustrading decorated with the ripe flowers of the hop plant, the tiled floor, and the decorative shields depicting Invicta – the symbol of the County of Kent, the home of hops.*

ABOVE *The elegance of the ironwork is almost flighty – there is a flavour here of Brighton.*

OPPOSITE *General view of the exchange showing the arrangement of the offices off the galleries.*

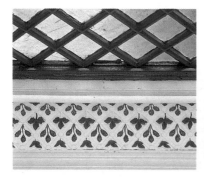

THE SOANE MUSEUM

Sɪʀ ᴊᴏʜɴ sᴏᴀɴᴇ (1753-1837) has been described in a manner that brings to mind a character from the Gormenghast novels of Mervyn Peake: 'tall and thin, with dark hair, a pale, excessively narrow face, bright, nervous eyes and a mouth tightly compressed above the long chin.' Contemporary accounts of his character describe him as a tortured soul. He had a happy marriage but a great many rows with his friends, and one of his sons attacked his work via an anonymous article published in 1815. This makes his architecture, what remains of it, all the more interesting because a Soane interior is the very essence of solace and peace. Such quiet emotion, slated where appropriate with grandeur, was spun from daylight. Soane was a master of composing interiors with outside light. But the reasoned order and even austerity in the forms reflect a discipline which, in his family life, expressed itself as autocracy.

Some of his best interiors were created for the Bank of England but today we have to recreate them in our mind via drawings and photographs since many of the rooms themselves were demolished during the rebuilding of the Bank (1921-37). Soane's particular compositional motif was the 'punching' of holes into solid forms; he made a lot of use of the pendentive dome – examples of which are shown here.

Soane was the son of a builder; he got himself apprenticed to George Dance and attended lectures at the Royal Academy. He won a Gold Medal from the Royal Academy and a travel scholarship to Italy. Apart from the opportunities for architectural study afforded by such a trip (it lasted two years) Soane also met other Englishmen on the 'grand tour' – they were wealthy, and later some of them gave him work.

In the 1780s Soane's fledgeling business secured several contracts for country houses; in 1788 and in the teeth of some strong competition, he was appointed Architect to the Bank of England. He remained Architect to the Bank until 1833 and this gave him position and status among rival architects and, more importantly, patrons.

No 13 Lincoln's Inn Fields, the house photographed here, now the Soane Museum, was rebuilt by Soane in 1812-1814. It seems to be the case with the interiors featured in this book that the passage from outside to inside is often a surprise – sometimes because the architect wanted to shock, sometimes because the designer of the facade is different to that of the interior. But the facade of No 13 Lincoln's Inn Fields prepares you for the

ᴀʙᴏᴠᴇ *The Breakfast Room showing the shallow pendentive dome – the effect of this delicate carapace punched through with a hole is to create a space that is both protective and rational. It is secure but not cosy.*

ʟᴇғᴛ *A bust of Sir John Soane himself. He bequeathed the house to the nation in 1837, instructing that nothing should be changed.*

ᴏᴘᴘᴏsɪᴛᴇ *The dome and a part of the collection of carvings and casts. The daylight from the lantern over the dome ceaselessly models and remodels the space as the day progresses.*

interior. It is bold and, although refined, it is assertive, icono-
clastic and above all it breaks with the consensus of the plain
brick Georgian Terrace.

What would the planners and neighbours have to say today if
an architect decided to so ostentatiously reclad his house in
stone and in such a narrative style? Perhaps the answer can be
seen with Charles Jencks' post-modern re-workings of his own
house in Notting Hill in the early 1980s (see page 198). Some of
his neighbours rather deplored the idea of his stepping out of
line, and making himself and his house publicly different.

The interior of No 13 consists of suites of domestic rooms
and also a complex linking together very private rooms – his
museum. These study rooms are dramatically lit. We have an
exciting series of transitions from light to dark, a chord of the
lumière mystérieuse to which no photographer can fail to
respond. The rooms are crowded with artefacts and paintings,
not in a clutter, but certainly a surprising contrast to the plainer
spaces of his public buildings.

The rebuilding of No 13 and the yearly growth of Soane's
collection happened at a time when Soane's personal life was
sour. Soane wrote a synopsis setting down his ideas about the
new museum, but written as if by someone writing from the

LEFT *The Library. This is a more
masculine room and the effect of the
red walls, heightened by the green
detailing, connotes a seriousness that
deepens as one moves from the
domestic to the museum spaces.
Each room has an emotional content
appropriate to its function.*

ABOVE *The South Drawing Room.
On the right is a 'verandah'. A
feature of Soane's genius for spatial
composition is his use of delicately
painted or plaster moulded line to
delineate areas of the wall and
ceiling to create harmony.*

future, speculating about No 13 and the museum. It ends by
saying that No 13 must have been the house of a great architect
'who suffered for his originality and integrity, and was abused
even by his own kin, and died of a broken heart.' His wife died
in 1815, his eldest son in 1823 and his younger son, a 'grimly
unsuccessful novelist, sank into a hopeless condition of Bohe-
mianism and embitterment.' During this period Soane
deepened and thickened his collection of sculptural and architectural curios and it is quite possible that the museum was an
escape as well as a tool to scholarly study.

THE LINLEY SAMBOURNE HOUSE

LINLEY SAMBOURNE was an artist who worked for *Punch* and lived in this house between 1874 and 1910. His grand-daughter, Anne, Countess of Rosse had many happy times visiting the house and has preserved her memories by conserving it as a *home*. The Countess of Rosse remembers 18 Stafford Terrace thus: 'The deep brown draperies and shadows were a little frightening but Stafford Terrace was a happy place. It was a house of perpetual motion . . . and now and then the little figure of the artist himself in his black and white plaid suit bounced down – with great gold watch in hand, to make it tinkle for the children.'

The home is full of things; hardly a surface is bare but the most striking aspect is the softness and mellowness of the light. The rooms are dark, as light has been filtered through decorated semi-opaque glass screened by vast drapes. The light touches the dark woods and deep greens, the reds and browns of the floor and walls. But the effect is not of Victorian gloom but of masculine, paternalistic conviviality. In some rooms there is a leavening feminine touch – the morning room, which was Lord Rosse's study, is an example because here the Sheraton and satinwood furniture adds a lightness of line that is accentuated by the heavier elements such as the gilded frames of the pictures and the rich elaborations of the William Morris wallpaper.

The Victorian sensibility liked to have things massed – like reefs of coral – it did not like to isolate objects for individual scrutiny. And so these interiors are like other aspects of Victorian art, advertising, and literature: consider the piling on of facts and adjectives provided by Charles Dickens. And certainly in Linley Sambourne's own political cartoons of the period we see a wealth of detail that no contemporary cartoonist (with the exception of Gerald Scarfe) would attempt.

All these details, all these facts create a sense of solidity and security and it is easy to see that, provided the people animating the house were pleasant, the home would have enormous appeal to a child. Nostalgia, of the kind prompted by this house, makes children of us all.

FAR LEFT *The harvest time glow in the hall and landings is the defining characteristic of this house.*

LEFT *There was a fashion in the 1870s for decorative glass depicting Shakespearian fairies – here are Ariel and (BELOW) Titania. We look on the Victorians as oppressively factual but they had a colossal streak of whimsy in them.*

OVERLEAF *The Drawing Room. The overall style of the room and the home generally is eclectic: it is a magpie accumulation ranging from Regency and Louis 16th pastiche to Japanese painted vases. As an artist Sambourne took a keen interest in other artists' works and there are several examples of work by contemporary Victorians such as Kate Greenaway and Walter Crane.*

Edward Linley Sambourne began contributing drawings to *Punch* in 1867. He was first called upon, so the Victorian Society who are responsible for running the house tell us, to fill in gaps and work on the decorative initial letters for a political column by Shirley Brooks. Apparently these initial letters became somewhat cuckoo-like in that they outgrew the column they were intended to introduce. The initials eventually took up three-quarters or more of the available area, and became, in effect, a second political cartoon. In 1901 Sambourne replaced the great political cartoonist John Tenniel.

It seems that Sambourne had difficulties in meeting his deadlines because he was a convivial, social man. Presumably political cartoonists, like journalists, need other people – and need the barbs of gossip – in order to get an angle on a person or an event. He spent a lot of time on research before making a drawing and the house is itself filled with pictures, reproductions and drawings. Given his great respect for detail and observation it is not surprising that he especially admired Albrecht Dürer.

The house in more recent years served as a kind of salon for Lord and Lady Rosse (the house passed to Lady Rosse, grand-daughter of Sambourne, in 1960). Thus you can find in the visiting book names of some famous modern image makers including Henri Cartier Bresson, the French photographer, John Betjeman, the poet who held the lamp for Victorian design when most people were rubbishing it, and Osbert Lancaster, the cartoonist and architectural writer. In 1980 the house passed to the Victorian Society.

TOP LEFT *A view of the Morning Room.*

FAR LEFT *Roy Sambourne's bedroom. Roy was Linley's son. The book illustrations by Sambourne are particularly interesting and include some of the best-known titles of the period such as Charles Kingsley's* The Water Babies *and* Three Tales *by Hans Christian Andersen. A very attractive characteristic of this house, more Edwardian than Victorian in some ways , is the abundance of lighter touches such as the delicately drawn floral frieze.*

LEFT *Detail of the bedroom's washbasin.*

BOSTON MANOR HOUSE

Boston manor house, built in 1622, and its pretty park, cling on into the 20th century in Brentford, a dispiriting part of London. The M4 motorway trollops across the grounds and when the wind is blowing from the east the air is split by the 747s lumbering out of Heathrow.

The architectural historian Nikolaus Pevsner believes Inigo Jones had a hand in Boston Manor's design. The Brentford local history society have issued a leaflet called 'A Royal Occasion at Boston Manor House'. Even if you are wary of the emotion of nostalgia, the following description of a visit to the house in 1834 by King William IV and Queen Adelaide is moving because of the contrast it presents to the wretched setting of the house now:

'The people were collected in numbers at Dr Morris's school, and they gave them good cheer. We then let the boys through the garden into the orchard by the flower-garden . . . We had our haymakers on the opposite side of the garden, and kept the people, hay-carts, etc, for effect, and it was cheerful and pretty. The weather was perfect, and the old place never looked better.'

Inside the house is interesting and rather lovable in a lumpy sort of manner. The main staircase is original and a shade pompous – a quality imposed by the sprightly carved heraldic lions that were added to the staircase in the 19th century. Ironically, in Brentford there are several semi-detached dwellings whose owners have sought to ennoble the entrance to their driveways with fake stone heraldic lions of a similar but less fine quality.

When the staircase was restored a trompe l'oeil painting was discovered on the right hand side which matches the balustrade on the left. Experts declare that the Jacobean drawing room is the best room in the house and it is the ceiling which grabs the attention. The plaster panels show figures illustrating the senses, the elements, and Peace and Plenty, War and Peace, as well as Faith, Hope and Charity. A state bedroom – for that honoured visit of a monarch – lies off the drawing room.

above *The overmantle of the fireplace in the drawing room; it is by Abraham de Bruyn and depicts the story of Abraham and Isaac.*

left *The ceiling in the Jacobean drawing room. The panels depict Earth, Air, Water, Fire, Light, Taste, Touch, Hearing and Smell, and they were designed by a painter called Marc Gheeraerts. The ceiling is dated 1632.*

above *The fireplace in the drawing room is shown here complete with an armoured steel grate, brass pillars and an ornamental cast iron back.*

opposite *A detail of the drawing room ceiling.*

ALEXANDRA PALACE

EVER SINCE the First World War some developers have been possessed by an urgent desire to pull things down and Alexandra Palace was more or less under the hammer in 1979. Today the 'Palace' is being aggressively marketed as a conference and exhibition centre. It has been refurbished and re-equipped for all those who need to dance attendance in the information age, the age of 'we talk, therefore we exist'.

An impressive building, a lovely park, but never a great financial success. It is the second of two palaces. The first was finished in 1866 but no one could afford to equip it and therefore the building did not open to the public until 1873. A fortnight later it burnt down. A second palace, designed by John Johnson, opened in 1875. With its amusements, race course and cricket field, the Palace was developed as an entertainment centre.

During the decades that followed the Palace changed ownership and lost money, and in the First World War it was a prison camp. During this period one of the central features of the Palace, the Great Organ, was vandalised. Not until the 1930s did restoration and repairs begin. In 1934 the BBC leased part of the building and built a large transmitting aerial. After the Second World War the Palace, which by then was in the hands of the Middlesex County Council, transferred to the Greater London Council – the body that wanted to knock it down in 1979, and which itself is now deceased.

Persuaded to hold off from demolition the GLC nonetheless got rid of the building by transferring it to the Borough of Haringey. Plans for modernisation were already prepared when ... the Palace caught fire. In a sense the fire opened up more options because, in the words of the local council, 'with the destruction of large areas within the Great Hall, a former skating rink and south front, much more use could be made of these areas and new technology could be incorporated.'

In 1988 the Palace reopened with a proposal for a 200-bedroom luxury hotel plus one of the most flexible and sophisticated exhibition spaces in the country. How things go in cycles. The Palace was born out of the 1851 Great Exhibition, that fulcrum of Victorian commercialism. Today in the so-called 'New Victorian' era, marketing pivots once more upon spectacular exhibitions, as well as the hard-sell conferences.

RIGHT *The vast expanse of the Alexandra Palace Palm Court. Grandiose yet functional, it is a true 'people's palace'.*

Restoration is expensive and because this is such a large building, and the purse is limited, those responsible for the refurbishment have edged cautiously towards completion preferring to perfect techniques in limited areas before continuing on a wider scale. The Palm Court, the central public space, has been put back into its original condition – as far as possible. Odd things have been discovered: Dr W. Peter Smith, planning architect for the restoration, says that in the course of recovering the Palm Court, it was discovered that the steels were sometimes as much as six inches out of true – possibly because they had been built that way. The restoration of the glazing is an example of the compromises forced upon the architects: to put back the curved glass and glazing bars would have been too expensive. But, unlike previous attempts, this time the refurbishment has been done with respect and thoughtfulness.

Elsewhere other restoration work has included the reconstruction of brickwork into the original condition and the repair and replacement of mouldings and decorative renderings. What is interesting about the policy of refurbishment as opposed to demolition is the opportunity it provides to compare new design with old. The equivalent 'people palaces' of the 20th century – the big, enclosed shopping centres – have a lot to learn with regard to good decorative detailing. In contemporary shopping centres one is treated to great efficiency, superior air conditioning and startling graphics, but the fabric appears insubstantial and any architectural features that are introduced look transparently like the pastiches they are. Whereas Alexandra Palace, although a very eclectic building and, even, a jumble of decorative ideas, is *substantial*.

In making Alexandra Palace arise (for the second time) from the ashes a balance has been struck between commerce and the broader desire to serve the public with fine workmanship. This is clearly a last chance for the building but thankfully commerce has been reined in enough to maintain the sense that this is still a 'people's palace'.

The balance of the economy appears to be shifting from the production of things to the packaging of ideas, words and images. This means a growth in conference and exhibition organising, and a welcome use is being found for the vast excesses of the late 19th century. These excesses – too much building, too much development, born presumably out of optimism – are now recycled for the soft work of modern times. The conference industry, which the Victorians might have described as ideally suited to the work-shy, expands it seems to fill the space available.

ABOVE AND TOP *The sculpted sphinxes in the Palm Court are by Mary Jane Opie. The British have a fondness for Egyptian style: they associate it with exotic spectacle.*

ABOVE *The restored capitals show a nice balance between austerity and ornament – no contemporary public buildings can afford this kind of graciousness.*

LEFT *It is pleasant to see lettering with serifs on the letters and a relief to get away from the ubiquitous 'airport style' letter face of public buildings. The gold, however, is a little raw.*

BELOW LEFT *One of the treats rarely commissioned these days as a decorative device is a terracotta frieze – clay, being so fluent, always gives an extra sensuality to any theme. There are 16 terracotta friezes, each depicting a scene connected with the idea of Empire and Trade.*

ABOVE *The Palm House – the roof glazing is not as it was but the compromise is acceptable.*

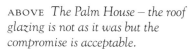

RIGHT *The Londesborough Room has these murals which, patently, ape the Roman style as well as indulging in the game of trompe l'oeil. They have been painted by Ricardo Cinalli and they have been based on works in the Church of St Andrea at Mantua in Spain by Alberti. Haringey Council supports the concept of art in public places and elsewhere in the building other contemporary murals are to be found.*

ST PANCRAS HOTEL

THE HOTEL AT ST PANCRAS STATION is, in the contemporary context, other-worldly: a brightly red brick building with masses of detail; a confection, something to pick at with the eyes. There are two high towers with ornamental turrets – the east end is 270 feet high, the west 250 feet high. The architect, Sir George Gilbert Scott, best known perhaps as the designer of the Albert Memorial which was under construction at the same time as this hotel, was also the designer of the Foreign Office in Whitehall (see page 46). He began designing the St Pancras Hotel in 1873, and the building was completed in 1878.

There was a building boom in the 1860s and the 1870s and hotels and railway stations featured prominently. Scott was commissioned to design the hotel by the London Midland and Scottish Railway Company, and it was first known as the Mid-land Grand Hotel. Scott did not in fact design the station, or station shed, which was produced by W.H. Barlow and R.M. Ordish. Barlow, a prominent Victorian engineer, was respon-sible for completing Brunel's famous suspension bridge in Clif-ton, Bristol. Architectural historians point out that the incongruity of Scott's elaborate fantasy set hard against the plain, functional station shed is an illustration of the dichotomy in Victorian culture – between facts, science and engineering on the one hand, and fantasy, covering up and theatricality on the other. The solidity of the iron and stone construction contrasts, for example, with the delicacy of the gold and russet stencilling on the staircase walls. Pundits commenting on contemporary Britain could point to a similar stylistic and cultural schism, the Lloyd's Building with its Robert Adam room being the most striking example (see page 39).

The hotel closed its doors in 1935. It was designed for 400 guests, cost £500,000 and took five years to build. After the war it was used by British Rail as offices from which it ran their other hotels (now sold off). For some years during the 1980s the hotel has been empty and neglect is wasting its bitty, bizarre interior. Plans are in hand to use the hotel as the centrepiece of a shop-ping, restaurant and cinema mall intended to outdo the hugely successful Covent Garden conversion.

The glamour of the interior reflects the confidence of the period but also the confidence in, and commitment to, public transport. Railways were things to be proud of and travel was an excitement; therefore arrival and departure in the capital of the Empire were significant moments.

LEFT *Starry ceilings and murals such as this – 'The Garden of Delight' – are balanced, occasionally, by the more formal gravitas of the solid pillar-and-arch architecture (*ABOVE*) upon which the romance is hung.*

OPPOSITE *The staircase is a marvel and goes to the full height of the hotel; between the wrought iron balustrades there are stone dragons. This is a romantic setting and the lighting is such that it creates a form of gloaming whose essence is part church and part Victorian fairy tale.*

THE BUSINESS DESIGN CENTRE

THE BUSINESS DESIGN CENTRE is the converted Royal Agricultural Hall in Islington. It was designed by Frederick Peck and engineered by a company called Handyside of Derby. It was constructed in 1861-2 and the central hall is vast – it has a clear span of 150 feet. All in all the space measures 384 by 217 feet.

For a while the building was disused but in the early 1980s it was converted into a conference, showroom and exhibition centre. As the Business Design Centre it opened in 1986.

It is a testimony to the growth of 'design' as an industry, one that is beginning to become as affluent, powerful and self-important as that of advertising. The Business Design Centre specialises in servicing the commercial sector – offices, banks, dealing rooms, hotels and retailers, and restaurateurs. It is a lively place, a little too well-groomed perhaps for those who favour the bravado of the original Victorian engineering.

The huge barrel roof is given a warm, theatrical glow by the use of uplighters and luminières, and its impressive architectural span covers 4000 feet of exhibition space, conference facilities and 120 permanent design showrooms. Fundamental to the 'concept' of the Centre is the interaction of transient exhibitions and permanent showrooms – a 'living showcase for developments in the design field' as businessman and brain behind the BDC Sam Morris expresses it. 'Design' here includes fine art galleries alongide the lucrative office systems companies. All work and no relaxation could make even designers dull – so the 'aggie hall' has its quota of restaurants and watering holes, ranging from the improbably named 'Peck Provender' to the ubiquitous mid-Atlantic Garfunkels. Nibbling food is a modern neurosis; there is such a variety of outlets that peripatetic chomping is now known as 'designer grazing'.

CENTRE TOP AND BOTTOM *The clarity of the Victorian design is amply demonstrated in the peripheral structures – and nicely refurbished by the new owners.*

ABOVE AND OPPOSITE *The engineering of the central hall is spectacular – the articulation of vast space with iron beams is always exciting. The hall's special quality is in the apparent delicacy of the iron work and the addition of the metal foliage that gives a fillip to the centre of the roof's arc.*

LEFT *The new entrance complements but cannot rival the original metal work. It is the difference between prefabrication and engineering.*

THE VICTORIA & ALBERT MUSEUM

IN 1988 THE V&A started to advertise itself with the slogan 'An ace caff with quite a nice museum attached' – it hardly did credit to the world's greatest collection of decorative art. But refreshments have always been important to museum visitors. Indeed, until 1939, the V&A boasted the most 'splendid ornate examples of government-sponsored interior decoration of the second half of the 19th century' – i.e. the refreshment rooms, known today as the Morris, Poynter and Gamble rooms. After the Army and RAF moved out after the war, these rooms were used as storage and were nearly destroyed in 1960. Now, after the restoration of 1974, they stand as exhibition pieces.

The history: in 1860 an extension to the original museum complex was started. This new three-storey extension housed a lecture theatre and the three refreshment rooms. In 1866 Sir Henry Cole, the Director of the Museum, placed the commissions for the interior decoration of the rooms. The green dining room (west) was offered to the new and relatively unknown firm of designers, Morris, Marshall and Faulkner; the grill room (east) to Edward Poynter, and the central room, designed by James Gamble, to the museum's own design team.

The walls of the Morris room are decorated with flowering branches and green wooden panels. The frieze around the ceiling depicts hares being chased by hounds through woods. The Gamble room is by far the most ornate, despite the practical choice of materials. The ceiling is clad with iron, as support for the lecture hall above, and was enamelled and painted to Gamble's design. The suite of rooms is completed by the Poynter room, which has large illustrative friezes.

ABOVE *The Gamble room with maiolica columns. The stained glass celebrates food and drink.*

LEFT *The stained-glass work is by Burne-Jones.*

OPPOSITE *The chimney-piece was designed by Alfred Stevens.*

OVERLEAF *The large tile panels illustrate the months of the year and the four seasons.*

THE SPITALFIELDS SYNAGOGUE

THE CENTREPIECE OF SPITALFIELDS is Christ Church, designed by Nicholas Hawksmoor (1661-1736), but among the lesser buildings are some beautiful Georgian houses such as No 17 and No 19 Princelet Street. These have some fascinating detail – and in what was the garden of No 19 there is a synagogue.

Fortunately Spitalfields is a conservation area and these two houses are now a study centre. The history of Spitalfields is a mixture of hope and misery, poverty and wealth. Three waves of immigrants have made their homes here over 200 years – first the Huguenots, whose trade was silk weaving and who as Protestants were forced to flee France in the 18th century. Then came the Jews from Eastern Europe, and today, partly because of the continuing and thriving textile trade, Spitalfields is home to a large number of Asian immigrants.

As Jewish immigrants settled during the 19th century they established what were known as 'minor' synagogues – congregations would meet in modified houses or in converted chapels. In 1865 No 19 was acquired and converted to become a purpose-built synagogue which opened in the autumn of 1870.

The rebuilding involved the creation of a vestry hall and a gallery for women, and the building of separate kitchens for milk and meat foods. Natural lighting was provided by a lantern skylight and windows , supplemented at first by gas lamps and then, in 1902, by electric light – which was quite advanced for the time. For a hundred years the synagogue had a major part in Jewish religious and community life but, in 1970, it amalgamated with the Bethnal Green Great Synagogue. This development was slightly curious in that the Spitalfields synagogue was simply shed; it was 'abandoned' lock, stock and barrel.

This was an advantage for the Trust when it set about restoring and repairing the two buildings in 1983: 'the synagogue was simply left standing, even its liturgical literature and archives, with vestments and furniture in their places, though deteriorating under a (now mended) leaking roof.'

Spitalfields began as a garden suburb and the relative wealth of the early occupants can be seen in the details such as the Rococo fireplace in the front room of No 17's first floor. The house altered when the silk industry began to decline – for when the master weavers could no longer afford separate workshops they withdrew to the attics in their houses – and towards the end

LEFT *One aspect of the workroom in No 17. The decay of a human habitat, its occupant presumed deceased, fascinates the living – the more so here, as the room is left not like a contrived still-life but frozen like a photograph – a last snapshot of a character.*

OVERLEAF *Nos 17 and 19 Princelet Street, Spitalfields have become* The Heritage Centre *– for the study of minorities. It provides a historical background to the area and, in particular, the succession of immigrants and their cultures. The long, narrow synagogue in No 19, lit from the lantern above, has an elegant gallery supported by slender iron pillars. The recess at the far end is where the Holy Ark was kept, the most sacred symbol of God's presence among the Hebrew people.*

of the 18th century a weaving loft was added to this house.

The last caretaker of the synagogue was David Rodinsky. He lived alone in the attic of No 19 and this room is to be preserved as the Rodinsky room. He was a second generation immigrant, whose parents were from Poland. In 1969, in his early 40s, he simply left the house and disappeared. Already there is something of a myth about this man: some say he was a learned scholar, others that he was, in fact, simple and possibly a little odd. All are agreed that he was a recluse. And there is even doubt as to whether he *was* the caretaker – the daughter of the Rabbi refers to him simply as a lodger. His diary remained and it is full of cryptic quasi-religious scribblings.

An obsessive man with a passion for languages, he had several dictionaries – Hindi, Welsh, Yiddish, Hebrew among them – and he kept newspaper articles about the Nazi extermination of the European Jews. Most of his personal belongings, his papers and passport included, remain and everything belonging to him will be put back as part of the preservation of the room.

ABOVE AND LEFT *David Rodinsky, a Jew whose parents had emigrated from Poland, lived in these rooms until 1969. Then he left everything and disappeared. The newspapers were the ones Rodinsky last saw before he left in 1969. The sense of mortality possessed by these rooms is powerful – a little sharp reminder of the proposition 'from dust to dust'.*

These rooms were formerly the work rooms of Monsieur Ogier, a Huguenot silk merchant and weaver. According to the literature supplied by the Heritage Centre, Ogier's drawing rooms were a centre for business deals, debates about French and English politics and for campaigns to protect the Spitalfields silk industry from cheap imports. Plus ça change.

DUDLEY HOUSE

DUDLEY HOUSE, at 100 Park Lane, was built for one man and 100 resident servants. The architect was William Atkinson; the patron John William Ward, subsequently the Earl of Dudley. Some have described this house as 'small and pretentious'; it is certainly a little overblown inside, but *small?*

Building began in 1824 and finished in 1827. William Ward became Secretary of State for foreign affairs but died mad. William Humble, the 2nd Earl of Dudley, and the house's next owner, was made bad tempered by his unfaithful first wife (she died giving birth to her lover's child) but he then married the very beautiful Georgina Elizabeth Moncrieff. Humble's irascible temper notwithstanding, he seemed keen to indulge the tastes of his second wife and rebuilt parts of Dudley House.

Georgina was interested in literature, painting – she sat for Sir John Everett Millais – and music, and under her influence the house became a centre for London society. Georgina entertained Edward, Prince of Wales, on several occasions. A picture gallery and ballroom were added to the house. The kitchens were among the largest in London and were segregated into three classes: the kitchen preparing food for the family, the kitchen preparing food for the senior servants, and the kitchen preparing food for the other ranks. Eventually, however, with the third generation of Dudleys, the money ran out: pictures had to be sold and the house let.

LEFT *The original staircase with a portrait of Lord Ward painted by Sir Joshua Reynolds (1723–1792), the first President of the Royal Academy of Arts.*

ABOVE *Here we see a portrait of Lady Ward, grandmother of the 1st Earl of Dudley, by Sir Joshua Reynolds.*

OPPOSITE *The balcony conservatory or loggia, of iron construction.*

MICHELIN HOUSE

THE MICHELIN TYRE COMPANY commissioned this building in 1909 and it was designed by a Michelin employee, François Espinasse – he was not, apparently, an architect. It is externally an outrageous building – a TV AM of its time – and the first drawings show Michelin men atop the outside turrets. These were later quietened down into 51 beehive hillocks.

The owners of the newly refurbished building, Sir Terence Conran and Paul Hamlyn, have published a celebratory catalogue in which they argue that the building is not to be categorised as any one particular style (take your choice from any of the following – Art Nouveau, proto-Art Deco, Secessionist Functionalism and geometrical Classicism!). Instead this was a company building, serving the propaganda purposes and values of Michelin who were seeking to build their commercial empire in England. This was a statement; it put the company on the map, literally and imaginatively.

The building also worked well as offices. As the catalogue states: 'From the grandeur of automatic doors, through to the detailing of an early telephone kiosk, the design of the building anticipated every requirement that might be made of it. For all its razzle-dazzle on the outside, the design of the interior of the Michelin Building must be recognised as a model of functionalism, affluence and stylish modernity.' People are not saying that about many contemporary London buildings.

The key image is *Bibendum* – the Michelin Man, the most famous image in tyre advertising and rivalled in motoring only by the Shell sign and a running tiger. Bibendum features on ceramic tiles, in stained glass and in mosaic. The building is a three-dimensional advertisement.

Conran and Hamlyn bought the building in 1985 and it has been both added to and restored in order to keep its integrity and make it commercially productive. There is a new Conran shop in the middle area of the ground floor, and there is a restaurant and bar designed by Conran and done out in materials that will age in keeping with the building – oak, ceramic tiling and marble. The major addition to the building are new offices designed by YRM Interiors – the internationally known architecture and interior design firm responsible for Singapore's underground railway design amongst other projects.

Perhaps we should be grateful that the Michelin building has been recycled for commercial use, rather than becoming yet another museum.

ABOVE *A pair of original doors with an unusual fusion of the organic with the geometric. The ad-hoc nature of the design provides character to this building.*

ABOVE AND RIGHT *The decorative panache is impressive – today no-one would design in a company's logo so permanently. Modern design has 'change of use' in mind. The propaganda here is mediated through decoration and craftmanship of great skill – so unlike the approach of the DIY and other self-advertising mega-stores on London's fringes.*

OPPOSITE *The Michelin building is a three-dimensional advertisement. On the floor, 'Now is the time to drink' – the glass contains sharp objects. Bibendum's point is that he won't be punctured.*

THE BLACKFRIAR PUB

THERE ARE SOME PUBS in the City that it is almost impossible to find empty at lunchtime. The Blackfriar is one of these, standing wedge-shaped on the corner of New Bridge Street and Queen Victoria Street opposite Blackfriars Bridge, its clientele spilling out on to the wide round pavement outside. Unless, that is, it is raining (not so uncommon), when the small inside bars become crammed full.

This unusual public house was built in 1875 on the site of the Black Friars Monastery. It is the only Art Nouveau pub in London and the outside, designed by Henry Poole in 1903, is decorated with attractive mosaics and small stone figures of mischievously grinning monks. Its ground floor area was remodelled in 1905 by H. Fuller Clark. The architectural historian Pevsner's opinion was that this is 'the best pub in the Arts and Crafts fashion in London'.

Today's regular hustle and bustle is a far cry from the peace and tranquillity that characterised the former occupants of the site. But we are constantly reminded of them on the walls inside, where bronze figures of monks are pictured performing their daily tasks. On one side they are carol singing, on another they are praying. Another portrays activities over the words 'Saturday Afternoon', while a frieze of monks above the bar informs that 'Tomorrow is Friday', a wish held by a good many customers at the beginning of the week.

At the far side of the main bar the beautifully figured marble arches lead into an inner sanctum, lined throughout with more marble, mirrors and superb gold and coloured mosaics. Yet more monks busy themselves on the upper walls. Sometimes, although the pub may be bursting out on to the street, this area remains almost empty apart from those eating at the several tables. Here they may consider the words of wisdom that encircle the sanctum: 'Seize Occasions', 'Haste Is Slow', 'Industry Is All' and 'Don't Advertise It, Tell A Gossip'. Another, 'Silence Is Golden', seems particularly incongruous against the loud hum of voices. Aphorisms and advice underpin pub discourse. Men, when liberated by liquor, feel free to take on all the world issues and then, sage-like, become intimate, breathing beerily into a friend's ear with 'a word to the wise, my son...'.

The Blackfriar is generally full of pinstriped City men together with a few women. There are no labourers. Like the area it inhabits, it only comes alive during the week, and is peacefully closed at the weekend.

ABOVE *Or* Festina lente *– make haste slowly – all drinkers know this.*

ABOVE *Victorian stained and painted glass was cheap and effective decoration.*

ABOVE LEFT *A savage little satire by Henry Poole R.A.*

ABOVE RIGHT *The interior is embellished with black friars in bronze. Critics argue that there is no historical basis for the connection of friars with conviviality which became a convention in the early 1900s. The pub was built in 1875, on the site of the Black Friars Monastery, and it was remodelled in 1905.*

LEFT *St Dominic, the Spanish priest (1170-1221) who founded the Dominican order.*

OPPOSITE *One does not need much detail when one is drinking and English pubs are boldly and broadly decorated in colours, marbles and wall coverings that soak up the nicotine.*

A GOOD THING IS SOON SNATCHED UP   INDUSTRY IS A[LL]

ABBEY MILLS PUMPING STATION

WATER AUTHORITIES are amongst the most important and conscientious of public servants – apart from seeing that we have safe drinking water, they also exercise important conservation and environmental policies.

The seriousness and pleasure with which they have taken their responsibilities has been traditionally reflected in the quality of their architecture and engineering. Many of the most elegant utilitarian buildings have been commissioned by water authorities (a tradition which still continues).

The Abbey Mills Pumping Station is beautiful and cathedral-like. But, lest one runs away with romantic notions, the scale of the building was determined by the size of the original beam engines – these were leviathans of huge proportions, their beams were 40 feet long and the fly wheels were 28 feet in diameter.

The architecture is both Gothic and Venetian in influence (appropriate given the connection with water) and the style was influenced by the teachings of John Ruskin who combined art criticism with social and economic theory – the visual vocabulary of a public building and how it expressed its purpose and the values of its service was therefore of considerable interest to him. In a sense this building, by Bazalgette and Cooper (engineer and architect respectively) is a piece of Victorian 'hypocrisy' – the graciousness disguises the fact that what the station deals with is sewage. But then heaven protect us from those who feel a building's function should be expressed too literally. The Victorians tempered civil engineering with courtesy.

LEFT *One might expect these doors to open up into a Venetian nobleman's house.*

RIGHT *The beauty of engineering and function knitted together in a decorative pattern that works both as architecture and in its fine detail. It is in the detailing of the metal structure that a synthesis between engineering and art has been achieved. Whether our contemporary determination to keep things plain is simply force of financial circumstance or genuine aesthetic choice is hard to tell.*

DENNIS SEVERS' HOUSE

IN A MUSEUM, in a stately home, in a house 'given to the nation' one expects and is expected to admire each and every artefact. In such circumstances it is assumed that everything old has its price tag as well as its provenance to the fore. This is not the case with this house, which offers one of the most unusual routes back to London's history.

The house is lived in – by Severs and his staff – but they live in proxy for a fictional family of the past. The family is called Jarvis, they are silk weavers and of Huguenot origin. Spitalfields, where this house is located, was a centre for weaving and also an area favoured by immigrants, first the French, then the Jews and today the Asians (and in particular, Bengalis).

When you visit this house you do so by appointment and you will be one of a small group of visitors; you will come, not to examine every object but to take in the atmosphere and make an emotional contact with a house that spans about 200 years of human occupation. The moments preserved in this house are nuances of human activity, and not simply the results of their labour. The rooms are equipped as they would have been at the time they represent, with furnishings and objects that often show their everyday use. Every room has the feeling of latent activity, you are made to feel that you have arrived just after the 'real' occupants of the room have finished dressing, cooking, eating and entertaining, or whatever it may be, and have moved on somewhere else in their daily round. There is no sign of electricity. The rooms are lit by candles, and fires still burn in the hearths. Smells linger – of flowers, or perfume, or mellow tobacco. If you allow yourself, you are transported into this family's life, immersed in the continuous stream of narrative that discreetly accompanies the journey through time.

The house itself was built in 1724, and its 'family' history takes us from that time to about 1919. We start in the dark cellar, and move upwards through the kitchen, the dining room, the elegant drawing room, up through the family bedrooms to the top of the house. With each move, we follow the family fortunes as they rise and fall, until we eventually find ourselves back again in the quiet East End side street, expecting to see a carriage turn the corner at any moment.

The whole experience – for it is an experience rather than a 'tour' – lasts over three hours. There are never more than eight people at one time, so it is not hard to lose yourself in the atmosphere. It is a complete contrast to the organised guided tours around more stately homes, with their stereotyped information about dates and noble connections.

FAR LEFT AND LEFT *Very little of the ornament, except the lace cloth, is handmade or precious. They are modest artefacts from factories – the industrial revolution of the late 18th and the 19th century brought dreariness but also cheap colour. The patriotism – images of Victoria and Albert – is more poignant when one remembers the immigrant roots of the inhabiting family.*

OPPOSITE *One of the qualities of the tour is the animation given to each room – potted plants, the hiss of the gas lamps, the burning of the fire and the flickering, live quality of the light that is thus created.*

TOWER BRIDGE

THE 800-FOOT-LONG TOWER BRIDGE is one of *the* tourist attractions; it is London's equivalent of the Eiffel Tower in terms of city symbols. Had such a bridge been built after the First World War, certainly after the Second, then it would have been impossible to combine engineering and 'fantasy' architecture in such a manner. The demand from engineers and architects would have been for more 'honest' engineering – to expose the structure, the mechanisms, and point up the modernity of the enterprise.

Perhaps. An earlier honest bridge higher up the Thames, the Hungerford Railway Bridge (1864), has been much reviled for its brutal ugliness. On the other hand, fine exercises in unadorned bridge engineering exist in Newcastle-upon-Tyne and across the Firth of Forth. But the setting of Tower Bridge is very special.

As everyone knows, it is close to the Medieval fortress of the Tower of London and the Victorians (who either invented, revived or renovated much that we take to be traditional) were conscious of the need to hold up the vision of the continuity of history. The bridge is, in any case, the first one a ship meets on the Thames. It represented the gateway into London.

Tower Bridge opened in 1894 after an Act of Parliament in 1885 had authorised its building. Parliament had, in fact, stipulated that the style should not be classical. It contains a raised footway which is 142 feet above high water and reached by stairs built in the Gothic towers. There are also lifts. Together the twin bascules have a span of 200 feet: bascules are the movable sections of the bridge and are hinged above a horizontal axis and counterbalanced by weights. Thus with a span of 200 feet (the headroom is 135) the engineering of the bridge towers and the power of the lifting gear needs to be muscular. On either side of the central span the chain suspensions are each 270 feet long.

The towers are steel framed in order to support the massive bascules and clad with stone. The hydraulic lifting machinery, made by Armstrong and Mitchell Ltd, was originally driven by steam and remained so until electrification in 1976.

The engineer of Tower Bridge was John Wolfe-Barry; the architect was Sir Horace Jones, although he died before the bridge was completed and thus its architecture is not as he had designed it in all of its details. Jones is also remembered for his design, built in 1865, of a new roof for the Guildhall (see page 14) and the arcaded Billingsgate fish market (1875).

ABOVE *The old steam boilers (no longer used). Steam used to drive the pumps which drove the hydraulics. The coal came up the river by barge, and was transported to the engine room in small wagons.*

RIGHT *The pressure gauges in one of the four control rooms – there is a control room on each downstream side of the two Gothic towers.*

OPPOSITE TOP LEFT AND LEFT *Two views of the accumlator tower which is located in the engine rooms on the south side of the river.*

OVERLEAF *Looking down the accumulator tower, flanked by a pair of 'pistons'. These are accumulators which stored power (in this case, water under pressure) until required.*

KEY TO EXTERIORS

PRINCE HENRY'S ROOM
Fleet Street
Holborn EC4

THE EXPRESS BUILDING
Fleet Street
Holborn EC4

FRED COOKE'S EEL & PIE SHOP
Kingsland High Street
Hackney E8

WHITEHALL THEATRE
Whitehall
St James's SW1

WYNDHAM'S THEATRE
Charing Cross Road
Leicester Square WC2

THE HOP EXCHANGE
Southwark Street
Southwark SE1

SIR JOHN SOANE'S MUSEUM
Lincoln's Inn Fields
Holborn WC2

LINLEY SAMBOURNE HOUSE
Stafford Terrace
Kensington W8

BOSTON MANOR HOUSE
Boston Manor Road
Brentford TW8

ALEXANDRA PALACE
The Avenue
Wood Green N22

ST PANCRAS HOTEL
Euston Road
King's Cross NW1

THE BUSINESS DESIGN CENTRE
Upper Street
Islington N1

VICTORIA & ALBERT MUSEUM
Cromwell Road
South Kensington SW7

SPITALFIELDS SYNAGOGUE
Princelet Street
Spitalfields E1

DUDLEY HOUSE
Park Lane
Mayfair W1

MICHELIN HOUSE
Old Brompton Road
South Kensington SW7

THE BLACKFRIAR PUB
Queen Victoria Street
The City EC4

ABBEY MILLS PUMPING STATION
Abbey Lane
Stratford E15

DENNIS SEVERS' HOUSE
Folgate Street
Spitalfields E1

TOWER BRIDGE
Tower Hill SE1

CHAPTER THREE

Private Lives

IN SPITE OF ITS PARKS and grand public buildings London is a private, introspective city. The innate guardedness of the British characterises all aspects of London life – private, official and public. Idiosyncratic interiors are often hidden behind unprepossessing exteriors.

It is obvious that the majority of buildings are private homes and London would only truly be 'revealed' if one were able to pick the locks and rifle through the belongings of the owners – for people do reveal themselves through their possessions and their decor. To an extent. Many people make their homes look like other people's – this is reasonable, people like to belong.

Some of the interiors revealed here are odd – not because their inhabitants are peculiar but because they are cross-grained; they are genuinely individualistic through choice, not circumstance. The poor souls who live in the interior of cardboard boxes under the arches in London also lead an interior life that is idiosyncratic, but seldom of their own choosing.

OPPOSITE *The London cab driver has a private life – with his family of other cab drivers. They meet and eat in little wooden huts and these tiny 'clubs' are as exclusive as any in Pall Mall. The wit and wisdom of the cabbie has long featured in Britain's satirical magazine* Private Eye – *if you wondered where the cabbies practise their repartee, now you know.*

ABOVE *The Speaker of the House of Commons in 1989, Mr Bernard Weatherill, at home in the Speaker's House, his official residence (see page 113). As a part of the Palace of Westminster the interior of the Speaker's House was designed by A. W. N. Pugin. One wonders how the referee of the Mother of Parliaments would cope chairing the cabbies shown opposite. He might of course even prefer their wit and wisdom – for a while.*

THE LUPTONS' HOUSE

OTHER PEOPLE'S OBSESSIONS are fascinating and in an age dominated by the paid specialist and the salaried expert the *amateur* appears as someone exotic, extreme, almost baffling. Lewis and Joan Lupton are amateurs in the definition of 'those who love their work' – they pursue art and praise scholarship for its own sake but they are more than hobbyists. Hobbyists hold no responsibility except to themselves, but amateurs are professionals without profits, and if they are scholars they must be as exacting as if they were being paid or else their efforts are self-defeating, even malignant. Lewis Lupton is not a scholar but a serious amateur historian and he has for years devoted himself to the compilation of a history of the Geneva Bible.

This compilation comprises 21 volumes. The Geneva Bible was written by religious scholars in the 16th century. They had fled from England to Geneva to escape the persecutions conducted under the reign of Queen Mary, who was pressing for a return to Roman Catholicism.

Lewis Lupton's history is written out in hand and illustrated by himself. Between five to six hundred facsimiles of each volume are printed and sent out to subscribers all over the world. Lupton is very honest – the history is a labour of love but only in part, he insists, a work of original scholarship because he has relied on research in learned journals.

There is a degree of eccentricity in the Lupton house. After all, it is an extravagant, almost vulgar idea to paint a version of the Sistine Chapel ceiling in a London suburban lounge. The painting may be seen, however, as an act of love. The Luptons are religious; Lewis Lupton worked for ten years on the ceiling – every day after tea.

There is an honourable tradition of serving God through work and there is something heroic in such a painstaking enterprise. It decorates the room and it was, as any act of creating religious art can be, an exploration of Lupton's own spiritual feelings. The great white ceiling was an inviting *tabula rasa* just waiting for him to work out his faith in emphatic, brightly hued particulars. He says 'there was no particular reason for doing it, only that the room just called for such a ceiling.'

Joan Lupton is also an artist, and a painter in particular of still-lifes. Both have worked in a way that has turned their home into a celebratory piece of art and the emphasis, unlike so much other protestant art perhaps, is on cheerfulness, life and optimism.

LEFT *The Luptons have painted several squares of the lounge windows with 16th-century coats of arms, portraits and insignia.*

BELOW *One of Lewis Lupton's landscapes above some pretty porcelain and some volumes from Lupton's history of the Geneva Bible.*

ABOVE *A baby grand piano, painted up with flowers and cheerful young faces and based on children of a family they know. Joan Lupton is featured on the lid playing a recorder.*

OPPOSITE *Lewis and Joan Lupton beneath the scenes of creation and crucifixion present a picture of strength, harmony and achievement.*

WESTMINSTER SCHOOL

WESTMINSTER SCHOOL is a cornerstone of the British establishment and like Winchester, respected for its academic achievements. Westminster, with its close links with Trinity College, Cambridge and Christ Church, Oxford, has two histories. In the 13th century it was a Benedictine foundation, owned by the Abbey until Henry VIII's reign. With the dissolution and then reinstatement of the monasteries the school was in disarray.

In 1560 the second tranche began when Elizabeth I refounded the school making it one of the three *Royal* foundations (Winchester and Eton completing the triumvirate). Elizabeth established the tradition of the Queen's scholars – there are 40 scholarships for gifted pupils. Scholars board in College and possess privileges such as attending the House of Commons to listen to debates. They are also present at Royal coronations where tradition will encourage them to shout *Vivat, Vivat, Regina* as the crowning is accomplished.

The longevity of the school can be read off from the bricks and mortar. College Hall, for example, was completed in the 1370s with a minstrel's gallery added in the Elizabethan era. In 1882 the school acquired the adjacent Ashburnham House, in its current form. It is claimed by some as the work of Inigo Jones but the preferred attribution is to William Samwell in the 1660s. This was the site of the Prior's lodgings (dating from the period of the Benedictine foundation) and the ground floor has the original 13th-century windows which the builders of the 1660s saw no reason to destroy.

LEFT *College Hall, 14th-century. Latin plays were performed here for Elizabeth I. The coats of arms belong to Trinity, Cambridge and Christ Church, Oxford.*

OPPOSITE *The restrained Neo-Classical Grand Staircase.*

BELOW *The Drawing Room of Ashburnham House with two Queen's scholars in Sunday Best.*

THE BRISCOES' HOUSE

THE BRISCOES LIVE IN a Victorian house, which has been gutted and redesigned by Brian Muller whose home it was. Muller studied film and according to *Architectural Review*, a journal which is intelligently cautious about over-intellectualising design, the interior of this house was intended to 'set up a participatory dialogue with the audience' – you make your own meanings from what is given to you. Muller apparently told the *AR* that he had wished to 'foreground the materiality' and treat the building 'as a constructed artefact with its own history revealed'. Sceptics might be forgiven for thinking that this simply means revealing the floor boards and the lathwork.

But, in fact, the results speak for themselves. The overriding recipe has been applied consistently – juxtapose smooth with rough, hard with soft, old with new, fussy with blankness, narrowness with space and, above all, outside with inside. For, this is a grand, eloquent piece of formal composition – a blockbuster flower arrangement. And although those ladies who dutifully create floral and twiggy compositions in churches throughout the land would look askance at the suggestion that they were 'foregrounding materiality' – that, in fact, is what they are doing. And there *is* dialogue – the designs engage one's imagination.

Muller's is a very knowing design: the contrivances are not especially 'clever' (not if you compare them with say a Butterfield or an Adam) but they are very effective. The use of the pink painted metal tube and mesh railing sets off the wood very nicely, contrasting not only surface effect but reciprocating one another's colour. The sparing use of older and time-worn fabrics gives areas of softness but the overall effect is not too soft, or sentimental. It is a very romantic house. It is also terribly English.

It is the English who, with the Italians, prefer things to look old, with references to the ageing process like decayed surfaces and revealed structures. But they seldom dare go after it in their own homes.

LEFT *In the end what makes a home is the quality of its light. The mellowness of this room is a perfect interior for London – it presents a continuous mixture of November and May, the two best months for light and colour in London. There is also a happy reciprocity between the engineering structures and the model sailing boats; a coincidence of metaphors.*

ABOVE LEFT AND RIGHT
The Briscoes' artefacts add another layer of meaning and text to an interior which is already a structuralists's delight.

OPPOSITE *The theme is structure and the use of the unadorned beam is a piece of modern assertiveness – the beam being the visual image which sums up modern architecture and modern engineering. Revealed in this way it is a bit of a conceit, but the ochre yellow prevents it being too obtrusive. The beam's unadorned presence is logically justified by the theme for the house.*

It is only now, as we move towards the 1990s that the ordinary English in the semi or terraced house is recovering from the post-war orthodoxy of *covering everything up*. Fitted kitchens and fitted bathrooms put a clamp down on untidiness. And year after year, from the late 1950s through the 1960s, hundreds of thousands of do-it-yourself activists all over the country followed the maxims and weekly exhortations of a TV DIY presenter called Barry Bucknell. It was he who seeded the notion that hardboard was the answer to every home decorator's dream: lovely doors were panelled over, mouldings ripped out, and newel posts sawn off – all in the cause of neatness. Muller's riposte, by deliberately exposing the processes of building and decoration, the permanently 'unfinished state', is amusing.

ABOVE *This is a studio over the kitchen. The floors have been cut into quite aggressively which allows trees to race up to the skylights as well as creating an interesting variety of perspectives. There has been a lot of artful 'framing'.*

FAR LEFT *The exposed lathwork has been filled in with pebbles and the wood has been sealed. The pebbles are there to provide density and sound insulation.*

LEFT *There are little formal cameos of textures and colours (with the colours kept within the same tonal range) set up like still-lifes.*

THE SPEAKER'S HOUSE

THE SPEAKER OF the House of Commons, assisted by three deputies, keeps order and umpires between the Government and the opposition (which often comes from the Government's own back benchers). Like the Lord Mayor of the City of London (see page 142) the Speaker has an official residence.

The first Speaker's House was erected in 1815 by George IV for his Speaker, Henry Addington. But after the fire which destroyed the Houses of Parliament in 1834, the Palace of Westminster was rebuilt by Charles Barry (see page 50), who commissioned A. W. N Pugin to assist him in the Gothic and Tudor detailing of the building.

Pugin was in love with the grand and the opulent: he was precocious as a child and had drawn up designs for some of the rooms at Windsor Castle when he was just thirteen. As an adult he was a passionate Gothicist who believed that Gothic was the only truly Christian architecture. He was spurred on in his obsession by the fact that the Establishment wanted Gothic (or at any rate the Government of the day had specified that a non-classical design would win the competition). Xenophobia militated against a European look for the seat of Government.

In the Speaker's House every detail of the interior, including all the furniture, was made to Pugin's designs – the results are typical of his rich Gothic style. Some of the furnishings were lost in the Second World War and before that a reaction against Victorian taste had resulted in the covering over of some of the elaborately decorated ceilings. Fortunately, the return to Victorian values of the last decade has resulted in full restoration. Many items of furniture have been re-acquired and restored.

ABOVE *A detail of the Corner Room showing the decorative panelling inset with the Speakers' coats of arms.*

LEFT *The Dining Room: note especially the fire surround and the ceiling – a feature of the ceiling is the Tudor rose motif, a favourite of Pugin's who was attracted by its organic symmetry.*

OVERLEAF *The current Speaker Mr Bernard Weatherill in the Corner Room, the main reception area. The Indian marble fireplace was restored in 1978; before that it had been painted over and the gilding covered in black emulsion.*

One of the most impressive rooms in the house is the Dining Room, which is hung with portraits of the Speakers from the early 19th century onwards. Speakers' coats of arms are set into the wood panelling which was crafted by Holland and Son. The contract was worth £5,381,13 shillings and 10d – *provided* they completed the work between August 1848 and January 1849. Failure to do so would have resulted in a forfeit of £50 a day. The whips were on to complete the work ready for Queen Victoria's State Opening of Parliament in 1850. The ceiling and fire surrounds are particularly extravagant.

Especially grand, however, is the State Bedroom, designed for new kings and queens to sleep in before their coronation at Westminster Abbey. It has never been used for this purpose although a visiting king has slept here. During the War the bed was lost; it turned up at an auction house in the early 1950s, went missing again and was rediscovered in a Welsh barn in 1985. The Victoria & Albert Museum restored it.

LEFT *The Receiving Room, which shares the ornate ceilings, fireplace and panelling of the Corner Room. The Gothic leaded windows are reflected in the mirror recessed above the fireplace. The table designed by Pugin is typical of him in that it is octagonal; apparently he never designed a round or square table.*

ABOVE *The State Bedroom and its wandering, seldom slept-in bed now restored to its proper place and function. The Royal College of Needlework made the drapes to Pugin's design using a loom specially built for the purpose.*

MICK HURD'S HOUSE

BAD TASTE DOES ATTRACT great interest. In the right hands, as with Andy Warhol, bad taste can become '*good* bad taste' – in the accepted late-20th-century understanding of art and taste in which 'good' means 'worth a lot of money'.

'Taste' generates heated argument on both sides of the Atlantic, where aesthetes opine that the majority have vulgar taste. But just as there are highs and lows in the history of fine art, so too there are peaks and troughs in bad taste art. There was a renaissance in the 1950s – especially in the United States.

Aficionados of bad taste would appreciate Mick Hurd's living room. It is the only room in the apartment (shared with Annie Curtis Jones) decorated in this fashion, but it symbolises the excess of kitsch that there is in the world. It is Hurd's altar to rampant vulgarity. Not only is the room filled with the most trashy and vulgar iconography but it is set against a backdrop of leopard skin wallpaper and tacky floral lino. Yes lino. Not vinyl!

But it is unwise to be too sniffy or too archly clever about these objects. You could, viewing the world slightly differently, remark that much of the interior of the Palace of Versailles is, properly considered, kitschy. In fact working class and aristocratic taste is connected by a taste for the glitzy, the overblown, the swollen and the over-elaborated. It is the people in-between, the middle classes, who are more censorious.

Many of the artefacts here were bought as souvenirs and gifts for other people – much of it is from abroad, much of it is plastic. There is a plastic pot made to look like a swan, various clocks, a star-framed convex mirror, and the artless pictures that appeal to sentimentality. And there, always prominent, is the television. The universal visually moving mail-order catalogue. The biggest single influence on our material aspirations.

LEFT *Mr Michael (Mick) Hurd at home in his creation.*

ABOVE *An altar piece at one end of Mick Hurd's living room. Over the years he has collected or been given religious knick-knacks by friends. The two armchairs, part of a three-piece suite, are still a standard part of most people's domestic decor. The*

1980s 'common or garden' domestic interior will look just as kitsch in 30 years' time.

OPPOSITE *The centrepiece of Mick's living room. A shrine to bad taste. Did those who dreamt up these artefacts think of themselves as designers?*

THE REFORM CLUB

Tᴴᴱ ᴍᴀɪɴ ʀᴏᴏᴍꜱ of the Reform Club are grouped around a courtyard which has a glass roof above it. The Reform Club (formed in 1832) was the club for the Whigs, the people who represented and argued for the desires of the industrialists and the dissenters of the 19th century. The Whigs provided the core of the Liberal Party. Past members of the Club include Gladstone, Palmerston, Lloyd-George, and Winston Churchill. The Club is also famous for the fictional character of Phileas Fogg (in Jules Verne's novel *Around the World in 80 Days*) who makes his famous wager at the Reform Club. Bertie Wooster was another fictional member.

Membership of this club, as with most clubs, is secured through seeking the sponsorship of existing members and once admitted the new member has the opportunity of joining one of the groups – the Political Committee, for example, or the Economics Group.

The building was erected in 1837-41 and was designed by Sir Charles Barry, who also designed the Palace of Westminster, and the club is next door to the Traveller's Club (also designed by Barry and completed in 1832). The Italianate architecture reflects Barry's main preference for Italian Renaissance style, although Barry was a congenial man, happy to oblige with designs to any architectural style that his client demanded.

This is not to imply that Barry was an equivocater; indeed, both these clubs present what was then a brave modern face. The architectural historian Nikolas Pesvner points out that Barry was an innovator – that the Traveller's Club and then the Reform Club were radical in their exterior design. Earlier clubs were in a Palladian style but Barry's clubs showed their modernity (and radicalism) by abandoning columns. A part of Barry's inspiration for the building came from the *Palazzo Farnese* in Rome designed by Sangallo, Michelangelo and della Porta.

Inside the style is dignified and spacious. The central court is especially admired as is the tunnel-shaped staircase which uses mirrors with great ingenuity. The impact of the bold interior is at once optimistic and confident; it is aristocratic but not imperious. It is definitely not, as is the case with some clubs, overblown in that pompous style associated with late Victorian civic architecture, where the ambience is stodgy like a lukewarm school lunch. The food, incidentally, at the Reform is reputed to be excellent.

ᴀʙᴏᴠᴇ *The Smoking Room is on the first floor and is directly above the Morning Room. The Corinthian columns add to the feeling of strength and permanence, while providing an intimate alcove.*

ʟᴇꜰᴛ *A bust of Charles Fox. He denounced the slave trade as well as advocating parliamentary reform.*

ᴏᴘᴘᴏꜱɪᴛᴇ *Apart from the huge number of volumes provided in the Smoking Room, the Club also prides itself on the quality of its journals.*

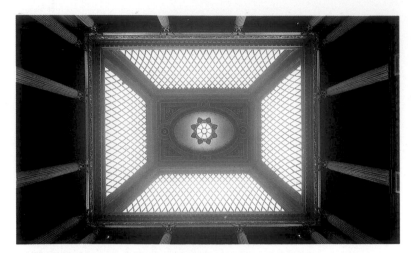

LEFT *Looking up towards the spectacular glazed canopy over the main entrance.*

BELOW LEFT *Looking across the enclosed courtyard or main entrance from the upper gallery.*

BELOW RIGHT *A view of the main court showing the entrance to the tunnel-shaped staircase.*

OPPOSITE *The terrazzo floor reciprocates the pattern that embellishes the canopy structure overhead.*

ROBERT PALMER'S HOUSE

THE ROYAL BOROUGH OF KENSINGTON & CHELSEA was inspired to build some 'Artist Studios' for local artists after the Second World War – perhaps in the tradition of some rural areas which presented World War I heroes with a small plot of land and basic cottage. Fleming Close was one of these small collections of studios and in 1966 one of its eight studios was taken by Robert Charles Palmer, a sculptor, with Ruby, his wife. At the mid-point of the country's most hedonistic decade to date Bob went against the grain. He says, 'In Richmond where we'd been living, we had all mod cons, but I needed something more primitive.' Ruby, however, was initially aghast at the absence of a bathroom. There was no hot water. She fought hard to share Bob's pleasure in the ample concrete floor. Yet their mutual loyalty and support won through.

Bob hates the word 'studio'. He says, 'This is a workshop by today's standards, a concrete garage with glass at one end.' The concept of the studio/workshop is simple but, in Bob's opinion, ill-conceived. The ground floor consists of four main studios, each with a small rear garden. Four smaller painters' studios occupy half the roof area, restricting the light reaching those below, while the yellowish brick wall opposite discolours the painters' light and obscures half the natural light.

The floor and ceiling are solid concrete, the walls are bare brick. Austere. Bob admits it gets cold in winter but there aren't many homes in which you can mix huge quantities of aluminous concrete – cement fondue – on the floor with impunity. He abandoned commercial projects some years ago and can no longer afford to cast in bronze, hence his greater use of concrete.

Theoretically Fleming Close is non-residential but Bob has always lived as well as worked here. Any early objections were forgotten and he could, in any case, only ever afford one place. Ruby shared it with him until her death in 1986; Bob mourns

ABOVE *A bronze of Ruby that Bob produced in the late 1930s. Of all the heads he made of her this one remains his favourite.*

LEFT *There are many swans around the studio – swans stretching, diving, preparing for flight, a pair with necks entwined – the swan is a favourite motif.*

OPPOSITE *Bob at work, building a head in clay. The saxophonist is also in bronze-coloured plaster.*

her every day. In this workshop he cared for her through eleven years of her mental illness having vowed not to let her return to a psychiatric hospital a second time. Without a hot water supply he kept her, himself and the studio spotless while he worked on the mass of figures and heads that still surround him. As he has grown older he has lost the desire to exhibit or sell his work.

Bob did not set out to be a sculptor. In 1928 he went to Berlin to be a writer. In Berlin a sculptor friend requested English lessons which Bob agreed to give in exchange for lessons in drawing. Soon his friend suggested that he try making clay models in his studio and Bob began his life as a sculptor.

He has been a socialist for 60 years and he believes the artist is always in the vanguard of the campaign to improve life for all. He has little patience with Mrs Thatcher and her version of England. 'Her heroes are estate agents. They describe the small corner where the sink is as a kitchenette, as I have put a stove and fridge there. When I'm gone they'll be describing that (the outside lavatory) as a Chelsea studio. Now that estate agents have annexed poetic licence to themselves, who needs artists?

ABOVE *Looking down the length of Bob's studio from the garden end. It shows the variety of methods he employs: he both carves and models clay which he casts in plaster and then colours to resemble bronze. He also works in cement fondue. The heads on the shelves are mainly of his daughter and grandchildren.*

LEFT *Looking the other way, towards the garden and holding centre stage is Jimmy, one of Bob's two adopted cats. In the foreground on the right is a carving of the Madonna and Child. Bob, 80 years old, is still sprightly. He can still hold his own in 'Finches', his local pub across the Fulham Road from the Studio.*

THE BRIDE OF DENMARK

THIS IS A PRIVATE PUB in the cellars of 9 Queen Anne's Gate, owned by the Architectural Press Ltd which publishes world-famous architectural and design magazines such as the prestigious monthly *Architectural Review*, the sprightly weekly *AJ (Architects' Journal)* as well as the *Designers' Journal*. It is used by the employees for coffee and tea, and to entertain contributors and advertisers.

At one time the hacks, the proofreaders, the layout artists and designers, those who clerked and those who sold advertising, trembled to the demands of one of the company's owners – H. de C. Hastings. Described by those who remember him as a brilliant but explosive man, Hastings used to summon his secretary with the less than sonorous blast of a hunting horn. He was alleged to be a recluse – an explanation that was offered for his disconcerting habit of never talking to you or any audience but instead declaiming himself at any nearby wall.

Hastings was interested in Victoriana. He thought that the old London pub was going to disappear for ever and so around 1947-1948 this pub was concocted. It is a real piece of tomfoolery and some people find it quite ghastly; others think they have found the root of all the trouble with modern British architecture. The fact is that had it been done today, exactly as it is, this school prefect's room humour would have been claimed as post-modernist commentary or irony.

In 1954, the *Architectural Review* published an account of its pub and listed all the ingredients that a British pub requires if it is to be a success: intimacy, intricacy, texture, decoration and lighting. With regard to intimacy it was opined that 'however large the pub the typical group of imbibers does not change much in size and wants to feel at home.' Subdivisions are a must. And the intricacy is needed because, with vista and mirror, a sense of intrigue should (must) be created. The aim is to make

LEFT *The pub was designed by H. de C. Hastings and stretches through the basements of three houses.*

OVERLEAF *There are three bars, filled with casks, pictures, engraved mirrors, bottles, and high-backed benches. The walls are covered with wooden panelling taken from former pubs and the floors are stone flagged. The mirror is replete with famous signatures, including Frank Lloyd Wright's.*

everyone feel secure and also that there is much more going on.

As a male bolt-hole the pub is generally quite extraordinarily domestic – men cannot subsist without a home nearby. Aesthetically the Bride of Denmark is quite how one could imagine the common room in Titus Groan's school at Gormenghast. You can see its appeal – it is reassuringly eccentric, and bolsters up everyone who drinks there with a sense of bohemian or intellectual exclusivity. It has a kind of Gothic rakishness which serves well the sentimental beery camaraderie of journalists. It is, perhaps, a mock-Victorian equivalent of Club 2000 (see page 150) – odd that the ideas do not flow so well in a tearoom.

Given the date of the *AR*'s own propaganda for its pub (the mid-1950s was when all the brutal designs for the world outside were being concocted) it is interesting to read the *AR* applauding the survival of crafts such as the painting of imitation wood and marble. Is that what they really believed after all?

Friends and employees appear, in the early years at least, to have contributed the occasional memento. There is also a mirror in the pub inscribed with signatures of famous architects, actors and sportsmen.

Why the 'Bride of Denmark'? There is a statue of Queen Anne (bride of Prince George of Denmark) outside.

ABOVE *Until the early 1960s this alcove was a bathroom. The engraved mirrors are originals.*

RIGHT *This poor thing was shot in 1909 in British Africa. He was rediscovered in an antique shop by an AP employee, brought to the Bride of Denmark and displayed in a manner suggesting he is more whole than he is. The trace of Cheshire Cat grin is a mite disturbing after a drink or two.*

THE RIDDELLS' HOUSE

THE PROLIFERATION of terraced housing that occurred in the 19th and early 20th centuries has proved remarkably enduring – and popular. True, many streets were razed to rubble in the redevelopment fever of the post-War rebuilding of Britain (and many terraces deserved to be demolished) but tens of thousands of terraced acres persist. Today it is the tower blocks that are coming down.

Fulham, West London, is a typical terrace land. The yellow-brick homes were for the working classes and the yellow-brick quickly went seedy black in the smog of coal-fired London. However, the Peterborough Estate was an exception. Here the brick is red, and instead of the roof line forming a monotonous band it is instead a lively line of gables and parapets. But it cost more. This was a better class of housing for people with rather more money.

In the 1960s and 1970s Fulham began to boom. It was seen as a middle class alternative to Chelsea (whose properties were by then very expensive). Fulham was full of potential. And the potential was seized: ground floor rooms were knocked through to assist free-flow living; attic and roof extensions sprouted and the more imaginative added conservatories. Peter and Phyllida Riddell were among the imaginative.

The conservatory faces south with a view down a narrow garden (which tapers and that which tapers increases one's sense of perspective and hence of distance – an illusion is created). The accumulation of well-tended shrubs and bushes, together with the trees overhanging from adjacent gardens, creates an atmosphere of rural tranquillity.

It is a matter of concern to some critics that the British do not like living in cities and it is this fact that encourages so many of the British to pretend in their small plots that they are in the country. But given the crammed-together ugliness of British urban sprawl it is hardly surprising that the spirit fights back with plants and murals. Anything for green relief.

Phyllida painted the mural which, viewed from certain points, works as a trompe l'oeil – a painting or decoration that gives an illusion of reality. Such paintings are beginning to prove popular with people seeking individuality as well as happy illusions in their home. But will, one day, a more sophisticated version of trompe l'oeil, such as holographic sensorama technology, help us all to transport our terraces to the Aegean or the moon? It's a distinct possibility.

TOP *Phyllida in front of her exotic painted mural.*

ABOVE *The Riddell's conservatory, a small oasis of oriental green in the heart of west London.*

OPPOSITE *A view down the carefully designed tapering garden (pride of the Riddells) offering them a fine sense of perspective.*

CHAMPNEY'S CLUB

CHAMPNEY'S CLUB is in the Meridien Hotel, Piccadilly. This old hotel, formerly known as the Piccadilly, used to be famous around the world for its lavish and exotic shows which starred not only people but elephants and ponies. The Piccadilly cabarets were especially prized and the music was broadcast worldwide. Sidney Kyte and the Players were among the cabaret bands.

The Piccadilly was designed by R. Norman Shaw (1831–1912) – a prolific architect whose other buildings include New Scotland Yard on the Victoria Embankment, the former home of the Metropolitan Police. The interiors of the hotel were by William Woodward and Walter Emden.

A hotel of grace, the Piccadilly was also a hotel of innovation. When it opened in 1908 people came just to see its lifts, lighting columns and the swimming baths – and moreover, there was hot water and a bathroom for every bedroom. These things were still luxuries in British provincial hotels in the 1960s.

The heyday of the show-time side of this hotel's career was in the inter-war period, but as a bastion of luxury, service and creamy indulgent escapism it has probably never been better. And that is saying something for, within a few years of its opening, the Gentlewoman's Court Journal described the Piccadilly thus, 'In this delightful haunt of the Sybarite a crowd of epicures and members of the "Smart Set" assemble to carry out the saying that it is a delight to "Live and Eat".'

Less ebullient watchers of the social scene in London of those times might have been minded to compare these epicures and smart-set Sybarites to the Eloi of H. G. Wells still topical *The Time Machine*. The Eloi spent their days in romance and sport. At night the Morlocks crept out of their underground homes to eat the Eloi. A social satire on the inequalities of British class and wealth, London certainly had sufficient people at the time with cause enough to copy the Morlocks. But revolution is, apparently, not the British way and Gentlewomen (and Men) are still holding court in the Champney's Club.

The hotel gained a new lease of life when it was sold to Gleneagles who then closed the place, renovated it – restoring many of the rooms to their former grandeur – and then sold it on to Meridien.

Champney's Club is situated in the basement which is fitted out as a health club; the swimming pool is in what was once a restaurant.

ABOVE *The jacuzzi, a modern luxury in a Roman setting.*

LEFT AND OPPOSITE *The main swimming pool of Champney's Club, a health club in the basement of the Meridien. There is also a lounge and billiards room. The entire interior was done out in 1985. The lighting is automated and is programmed to fulfil different lighting sequences.*

THE CHELSEA ARTS CLUB

IN 1991 THE CHELSEA ARTS CLUB will be a century old and Ralph Steadman, the artist, told the *Tatler*: 'It's the only club I know that has gone from bad to worse and is still the best in London.'

Towards the end of the 19th century a lot of artists had settled in Chelsea because it was cheap and they found each other's company congenial. Some of them began meeting in a pub and then rented a floor in 181 King's Road and formed a club. In 1902 they moved to the current premises at 143 Church Street.

Founder members included Whistler, Steer and Sickert and the honourable aim of the club was 'to encourage and advance the cause of Art and to provide facilities for social exchange between artists practising the graphic and plastic arts.'

In practice this meant having a good time – plenty of dinners, getting drunk, having bloody good rows and scandalous balls. The Annual Chelsea Ball was a thing of notoriety.

The Club is enjoying a renaissance thanks to Dudley and Mirijana Winterbottom who used to run a restaurant in Oxford and who rescued the Arts Club from its decline of the 1970s. Today, those who are fortunate enough to be members are proud of the privilege. There is a long waiting list and the artists have plenty of contemporary anecdotes to pass on. Male artists in particular are always proud of their emotions and their ability to fight and make up.

The enduring and endearing message about the club is its warmth, friendliness, good food, funny jokes, and a lovely garden. The club has bedrooms for members and members have their own keys so that it must feel like an extension of one's own home – which in itself runs against the orthodoxy of stuffier Pall Mall clubs.

Several changes have been instituted which bring the Club back to its roots: there are regular lunches for artists so that younger members can get to know and exchange ideas with older artists; there are regular exhibitions of members' work and there are special one-artist shows in which a small collection of the artist's work is borrowed from outside the club and presented as a small exhibition. Member artists thus so far presented include Ruskin Spear RA and Sandra Blow RA.

It is wholly appropriate that there is a two-tier membership – only practitioners of the fine arts are full members, the rest are associates. Such an arrangement keeps faith with the instincts of the founders.

TOP *One of the three dining rooms with a selection of the paintings in the Club's permanent collection, including an Arab street scene by Henry Bishop and a portrait by Frederick Brown.*

ABOVE *The main table of the dining room can seat 30 people.*

OPPOSITE *The billiards section of the main bar. It is here that the special, one-person shows are organised by Dudley and Mirijana Winterbottom.*

OVERLEAF *A secluded alcove in the dining room. On the wall are framed covers of the celebratory menus from annual dinners in the past, drawn by various members of the Club.*

A CHELSEA HOUSEBOAT

RECYCLING IS AN interesting phenomenon in London these days. This houseboat, worth several hundreds of thousands of pounds, is built on the hull of an old freight boat. The hull used to carry rubbish down the river. Today it is the foundation of luxury and is moored off Cheyne Walk in Chelsea.

The *Blackhoe* can command a huge selling price because of its position, its superb fittings and the fact that it is an *interesting* property. The views it commands are among the best on the Thames (the very best view the Thames offers is at the Isle of Dogs where you look across the sulky old water to the Royal Naval College at Greenwich, see page 179). But the *Blackhoe* has views of the Battersea and Albert Bridges and the more recent, somewhat quixotic, Chelsea Harbour development.

The original owner of the *Blackhoe* was a millionaire businessman from Sweden: he wanted an interior that was simple but not austere. He wanted that Scandinavian restrained luxury that derives its character from the careful selection and gentle use of good quality materials.

Natural materials in particular provide most of the decorative aspects: throughout the interior the flooring is in thin pale strips of ash, the Scandinavian stove (which is coal-burning) sits on a granite slab and the rugs, upholstery fabrics and curtains are woven from wool or cotton. However, restraint has been the keyword – there is enough soft covering to make one comfortable but not so much that the boat is turned into one of those dreadful bijou interiors beloved of folksy river or fairground itinerants.

The interior designers were Julian Powell-Tuck and Mark Lintott of one of Britain's best known architectural design practices; they are specialists in the new modernism (a more humane

ABOVE *Looking towards the end of the main living area with furniture upholstered in Greaves-Lord fabrics (she also designed the specially commissioned woollen rug).*

LEFT *General view of the living and entertaining area. The box in the foreground has a hinged top and doors which open to reveal the staircase which leads down to the* bedrooms. *Apparently this box is also intended to echo the structure of a container ship (boxes on steel hulls).*

OVERLEAF *This is a big boat. On the walls you can see rectangular frames standing proud of the main surface. These floating frames are a decorative feature adorned with Greaves-Lord paint treatment.*

version of the style deplored by the Prince of Wales). The river-Romany look would be anathema to these designers.

Powell-Tuck and Lintott drew their inspiration, sensibly, from traditional river vessels. They sought to maximise the advantages of natural light and make full use of the wondrous views. The light, of course, is marvellous because being so close to the water one has the excitement of that special sheen and, sometimes, the magic glinting of the sun on the choppy surface.

The walls at either end of the boat are almost entirely glazed and rows of smaller windows along the sides puncture the interior with the biting light. The central living space is roofed over with a skylight. One is adrift in a watercolour; an odd but engaging experience in London.

The other designer who has contributed greatly to the success of the interior is the textile artist Sally Greaves-Lord, one of Britain's most talented interior design artists, post-graduate of the Royal College of Art and well-known for her 'architectural' work. She has also applied special paint treatments to some of

the fittings. For example, the staircase box had paint applied in layers, which were then rubbed down to make textural effects. The design is completed by pencilled borders. Greaves-Lord is one of the new generation of textile designers. She works directly on the cloth, and has thus merged the traditional craft of the fabric printer with the avant garde of experimental painting.

BELOW *The master bedroom at the river end of the houseboat. There is also an en-suite bathroom and sauna. The design of the duvet cover gives the effect of rippling water, shades of Hockney turned to Thames.*

RIGHT *The 'container box' over the steel staircase in a partially open position – there is a hint in this of a Giorgio Morandi painting. Everything is protestant and contrived like a pedagogic exercise in still-life painting.*

ST PAUL'S LIBRARY

THE LIBRARY CHAMBER at St Paul's Cathedral is rarely open to the general tourist; it is a large space with a high, vaulted, brick and plaster ceiling. The exciting aspect of this room is the quality of its carving.

The 20th century has not yielded really good carving: the skills do not exist that can create intricate form by taking away rather than adding to or modelling a material. Carving is fiendishly expensive and time-consuming and it is no surprise that over the years the demand for ornament that looked carved resulted in an explosion in the business of plaster mouldings – much cheaper and capable of being extremely fine (think of the 18th century, for example). But in this lovely room we are not looking at short cuts but fine stone and oak carving.

The eight stone pilasters, four on the north side of the gallery and four on the south side, were carved by a team led by a master mason called William Kempster. A guide to the Library explains that the craftsmanship is so fine that one expert, writing in a book about Sir Christopher Wren's architecture, thought it was plasterwork. The stone carvings are replete with inkwells, sheaves of corn, quill pens and the like; they are reassuring, contemplative, easy to understand and light-heartedly secular.

The gallery and its balustrade, the book shelving and the wood-block floor, were constructed under the supervision of Christopher Wren's master joiner, Sir Charles Hopson.

The Library contains 16,000 books – a collection gradually built up since the fitting out of the room in 1708 and 1709. Naturally a number of the works are very valuable, but books, like buildings, demand maintenance and each year students from the Camberwell School of Art and Crafts spend some weeks cleaning books, and treating them with preservatives.

The librarian makes clear that this is a working library and of interest to scholars, especially in theology and ecclesiastical history. The St Paul's Library contains an important collection of manuscript volumes. Some are placed outside the Library – for example, the Treasury in the crypt contains a 10th-century book of medicine and a 15th-century French book of hours.

A proposal made in the late 1960s to remove the books to the University of London's library was rejected because it was decided that 'to remove the bookstock from the chamber designed to house it would be to impoverish both'. The books would be most useful, it was decided, in the place to which many of them related through provenance or subject matter.

ABOVE *The marble-surrounded fireplace is the original and the portrait above the fireplace is of Henry Compton. Compton had been Bishop of London for the 35 years of the rebuilding of St Paul's. The sitter holds a drawing with the caption –* Combustam inveni. Extructam reliqui. *'I found it burnt. I left it rebuilt.'*

LEFT *Detail of the fine stone carving by William Kempster and others.*

OPPOSITE *The full magnificence of the room – the books on three sides with the three big windows on the south side.*

THE SHARPES' HOUSE

PHIL AND MARY SHARPE have lived in this house in Stanmore since 1937. They bought it new for £900 and the house, although carefully and proudly maintained, has not been altered. Coming from a generation unaccustomed to synthetic warmth the Sharpes have seen no need to install central heating. During the winter, the large electric fire is removed in favour of the traditional cosiness of a real coal fire.

Unlike many of their neighbours, the Sharpes have also felt it unnecessary to knock their two ground floor rooms into one, preferring the intimacy of the original dimensions. In fact, all the rooms are quite small but separate, including the tiny toilet and bathroom. Compared to the overcrowded nature of much rented accommodation in the earlier part of the century, the prospect of this relative privacy was a treat. The original plan here has hardly changed.

This is a typical piece of ordinary London suburban housing – a three-bedroomed brick-built villa, the result of speculative building between the wars.

A lot of London's suburban housing to the north of the Thames was dependent upon the extensions of the London Underground, and building developers were happy to buy greenfield sites and develop estates knowing that London Transport would follow them.

Suburban housing built in the 1920s and the 1930s is regarded by many people, especially foreigners, as a series of long blots on the landscape. The problem was that neither the planning laws nor people's sensibilities were sensitive enough and, in any case, the buildings sprang up so quickly. So much green land was ruined almost before people realised what was happening.

Despite this, the insides of these houses are very decent. They were built for careful and cautious people who worked hard and whose families, especially after the Second World War, formed a good, solid core of prosperity. They and their children enjoyed the fruits of their own work and the benign help of the welfare state, the 1944 Education Act and the new democracy of materialism.

One of Phil and Mary's children passed her 'A' levels and got to university – the first in the family to do so. Meanwhile the parents acquired a first car and television set in the 1950s and then began travelling abroad for holidays in the early 1960s. It is a story of growing prosperity that is repeated a myriad times over throughout Britain.

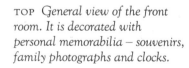

TOP *General view of the front room. It is decorated with personal memorabilia – souvenirs, family photographs and clocks.*

ABOVE LEFT *The ubiquitous telly provides a good mantelpiece. The decor is elaborated everywhere with patterns and flowers; there is a lot to excite the eye. The English living room is like the English garden – very tidy but agitated.*

ABOVE RIGHT *The hall of mirrors.*

OPPOSITE *The big electric fire animates and warms the eyes because the coal effect light is switched on even when the heating elements are off. (In the US, it is said, you can have a video of a 'real fire' and play that on the TV as a living fire substitute.) The mantelpiece and fireplace have been built up into a veritable altar.*

THE MANSION HOUSE

THE OFFICIAL RESIDENCE of London's Lord Mayor, the Mansion House was designed by George Dance the Elder, Surveyor to the City of London 1735-68, and father of Dance Younger. He also designed a number of churches in the first half of the 18th century. Each is in a classical style and most are somewhat dismissed by architectural critics as 'ungainly' and 'provincial'. However, most concede that the state rooms at the Mansion House are sumptuous.

While it would be unfair to describe the architect as working from reference books, it is very likely that he studied books such as Kent's *Designs of Inigo Jones* and *Builders' Guides* written by craftsmen such as Isaac Ware, William Halfpenny and Abraham Swan. Such reference would help him to render the details correctly. Even so, Dance the Elder raised eyebrows because he gave the building a double attic, and a print of 1750 shows the Mansion House looking as though one 'Roman' building had been unceremoniously dumped on top of another. Later modifications reduced this unfortunate effect.

One of the main interior features of the building is the long view you can achieve on the first floor through the Hall and Saloon into the Egyptian Hall. The Egyptian Hall is the principal room in the building. The special feature of this room is the barrel vaulted ceiling – it is a later addition and a masterpiece of colouring.

The description 'Egyptian room' comes from Marcus Vitruvius Pollio , a military engineer to Julius Ceasar. Vitruvius wrote a ten-volume account of classical architecture, and the influence of this work on architects and architecture since then has been immense. The term Egyptian is applied to a hall which has a row of columns and windows above the cornice.

The first floor Saloon is impressive but the most notable features are the gilt and crimson upholstered armchairs which were a gift from the citizens of London to celebrate Nelson's victory in 1798 at the Battle of the Nile. This cool room has no windows on to the outside world, but doors lead off into elaborately ceilinged antechambers that run along its length on both sides. The Saloon is used for some official dinners and shows, such as fashion shows (as was the case when researching this book – the Saloon was bedecked in palms and flowers with a catwalk through the centre and into the Egyptian Hall to the Lord Mayor's table). A gallery runs around the sides of the hall, from which musicians often entertain guests below.

ABOVE *The Egyptian Hall has 23-carat gold leaf decoration – seen here to great effect on the detailing of the Corinthian columns.*

LEFT *A detail from* The City Window *at the eastern end of the Egyptian Hall. It is by Alexander Gibbs and shows Edward VI entering the City after his Coronation in 1547.*

OPPOSITE *The Saloon with the roof designed by George Dance the Younger, whose father originally designed the building.*

OVERLEAF *The retiring mayor, Sir Greville Spratt, in his residence.*

KEY TO EXTERIORS

THE CABMAN'S SHELTER
Warwick Avenue
Maida Vale W9

THE LUPTONS' HOUSE
Chiswick W4

WESTMINSTER SCHOOL
Dean's Yard
Westminster SW1

THE BRISCOES' HOUSE
West Hampstead NW6

THE SPEAKER'S HOUSE
Palace of Westminster
Westminster SW1

MICK HURD'S HOUSE
Essex Road
Islington N1

THE REFORM CLUB
Pall Mall
St James's SW1

ROBERT PALMER'S HOUSE
Chelsea SW10

THE BRIDE OF DENMARK
Queen Anne's Gate
Westminster SW1

THE RIDDELLS' HOUSE
Fulham SW6

CHAMPNEY'S CLUB
Piccadilly
St James's W1

THE CHELSEA ARTS CLUB
Old Church Street
Chelsea SW3

'THE BLACKHOE'
Cheyne Walk
Chelsea SW10

ST PAUL'S LIBRARY
St Paul's Cathedral
The City EC4

THE SHARPES' HOUSE
Stanmore, Middlesex

THE MANSION HOUSE
The City EC4

CHAPTER FOUR

The Decorative Tradition

THROUGHOUT EUROPEAN HISTORY there have been attacks on the immorality, ungodliness or base vulgarity of decoration.

It is true that sometimes decoration has been used to cover up mistakes, shoddy workmanship or cheap materials. In this century the most famous attack was made by an Austrian architect, Adolf Loos, who linked a liking for decoration with poor taste and debased tendencies. But this was just theory. In practice not even Loos could resist decoration.

In spite of the consistent attacks by Cromwellian style and taste arbiters who have sought to rid our interiors of even the humblest picture rails, we see today a triumphant return of decoration. The skills have yet to be rebuilt to the point where they can match the achievements of the previous centuries, but popular opinion has forced the re-flowering of the decorative tradition. Even at the height of modernism when the fashion for plainness was exploited commercially as a way of saving money there were men and women who continued to embellish the world. Thank heavens.

OPPOSITE *St Paul's Cathedral (1675–1711), designed by Sir Christopher Wren and finished when he was 79. One's first impression is of cool, rational massiveness but there are passages of great decorative richness in the dome, at the crossing and the choir stalls carved by Grinling Gibbons.*

ABOVE *One of the many examples of carving in the Tower House (see page 172). Contrary to what people have said – including eminent men like John Ruskin and William Morris – Victorian craftsmanship has probably never been equalled, let alone bettered. One of the skills so amply demonstrated in this detail is that of carving – this skill is in terminal decline in our own country.*

LEIGHTON HOUSE

GEORGE AITCHISON, ARCHITECT (1825-1910) was one of the minor masters of High Victorian Gothic and a master of decoration. But Leighton House has a Classical rather than Gothic exterior and is indicative of Aitchison's taste for Italianism. The red brick exterior gives very little indication that inside there is a wealth of Eastern and Moorish-inspired design and decoration.

It was built between 1865-79 (it evolved and grew) and was commissioned as a home and studio by Lord Leighton, who assisted his friend Aitchison in the design. Leighton was a painter who became President of the Royal Academy and enjoyed much success. His taste in painting was literary; he believed in exact representation and great detail. Leighton's painting *And The Sea Gave Up The Dead Which Were In It* was one of the 67 pictures which constituted the original gift of Henry Tate to what is now the Tate Gallery.

Just as contemporary designers use their offices to project the right cultural image to impress, reassure and flatter their clients, so too did artists in the Victorian era. As other observers have noted, this house was designed with a back entrance for the models, promenades for the delectation and relaxation of the clients, and a generous and luxurious studio.

Among his friends were several who were prominent in the Arts and Crafts movement of the time. For example, William de Morgan the ceramicist, whose work features in Debenham House (see page 182), designed new tiles for the Arab Hall which was added in 1877-79. The Arab Hall, also created by Aichison, is based on the Muslim Palace at Palermo and was designed as a setting for Lord Leighton's collection of tiles which had been gathered from Cairo, Damascus and Rhodes. The tiles cover the walls and take their place in a room which has a cupola (a domed turret) with stained glass lights, an elaborate marble mosaic floor, a fountain and Cairene lattice-work in the alcoves.

It is, literally, a fantastic room, but one with delicacy and grace. Apart from William de Morgan's contribution, the sculptor Edgar Boehm carved the capitals and Walter Crane designed a mosaic frieze. Crane was the leading spokesman for the Arts and Crafts movement, and a designer of pottery, textiles and wallpaper. Leighton House is now, appropriately, a museum and art gallery.

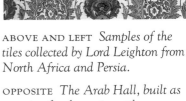

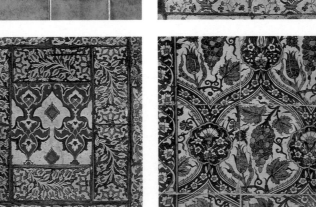

ABOVE AND LEFT *Samples of the tiles collected by Lord Leighton from North Africa and Persia.*

OPPOSITE *The Arab Hall, built as a setting for the antique tile collection. This space is rarely crowded with visitors. One of the special qualities of the room is its responsiveness to sound; the echo of one's footfall and the gentle play of the fountain act as an aural pivot to the visual kaleidoscope.*

CLUB 2000

THE HISTORY OF ARCHITECTURE (and design) is filled with stories of awkward clients and obdurate architects – the latter insisting that they know best and getting upset if their clients 'compromise' their work. But the Crucial Design partnership of Joshua and Kitty Bowler seek to provide what the client wants.

Club 2000, a Crucial Design commission, is intended for the glitzy young – men and women who are in one of the media and advertising trades or in the music business. Such people, hard-working, ambitious and bright, nonetheless like the *frisson* of rebellion. Hence the anti-design style of the 1980s is a fashionable favourite. This style probably had its roots in the Punk movement of the 1970s. And there is another factor. The English (being a generally ugly race) are tolerant of and even excited by ugliness. Hence the English, more than any other European nation, seem to take the scrap and junk aesthetic very much to heart.

It is also instructive to compare these decorations to the work of William Burges (see page 172) because, in the late 20th century, if we want elaborate ornament, then we have to make do with ready-made, mass-produced bits and pieces – plastic moulded figures, bits of cars and the like – which, whammed together, create a knobbly pastiche of 19th-century craftsmanship. The jumpy, erratic 'cut and splice' feel to the design is appropriate to the music business clientele, especially that part of it brought up on videos – the setting here is like a montage of video pictures.

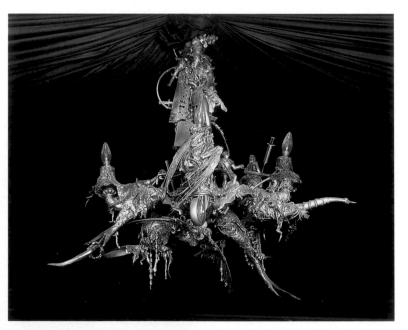

ABOVE *The composite chandelier is by William Longden.*

FAR LEFT *The stools are composed out of recycled motor engine gear-boxes, designed by Rob Lee.*

LEFT *The woman emerging from the wall is by Robin Cooke. The design of Club 2000 has a hint or flavour of decadence, but it is a nice, safe decadence that does not have the rawness of reality.*

OPPOSITE *The car coming through the wall is a 1980s de rigueur device – as well as being a Triumph 2000.*

CHISWICK HOUSE

CHISWICK IS ONE of the nicest of the 'inner' London suburbs. Until the middle of the last century it was rural and it was the railway rather than the development of industry which forced its growth. One of the centrepieces is the Palladian villa Chiswick House, designed by the 3rd Earl of Burlington, Richard Boyle. It was built between 1725-29 (some authorities say 1723-29) and was not Burlington's residence, but used for entertaining and to house his library and art collection.

Burlington was at the centre of the early to mid-18th century cultural and intellectual elite – his friends included the poet and satirist Alexander Pope, the philosopher Bishop Berkeley and George Frederick Handel the composer. There are especially pertinent lines from Pope that refer to Chiswick House:

> *Erect new wonders and the old repair;*
> *Jones and Palladio to themselves restore*
> *And be whate'er Vitruvius was before.*

On the outside the building is grand, the austerity of its geometry softened by a frieze of trees – the inspiration for the architecture is Palladio's *Villa Rotonda* outside Vicenza. There are interesting touches such as the obelisks which contain chimneys. The interior has been influenced by Inigo Jones. The original approach into the interior is dramatic – you go down a passage into the bright, tall central salon which has an octagonal dome. Off the central salon there are the entrances to the main rooms. There are four tightly spiralled staircases in each of the four main angles of the salon. Lord Burlington's protégé, William Kent, did much of the interior design, in particular the composition and decoration for the ceilings and chimney pieces. The rooms were restored in the 1950s by the Ministry of Works, and much of this restoration has a cold quality which was 'probably appropriate to the designer's didactic intentions'.

Kent also worked with Burlington in landscaping the grounds. Over the years, as the house passed through the Devonshire family, the gardens were added to. Although the gardens have fallen into disrepair, there remain statues of Pompey, Caesar and Cicero, an Ionic temple, two obelisks, an avenue of urns and sphinxes and a conservatory designed by Samuel Ware.

Apart from the house of the Queen's scholars of Westminster School (see page 108), Chiswick House is the only remaining building designed by Lord Burlington in London.

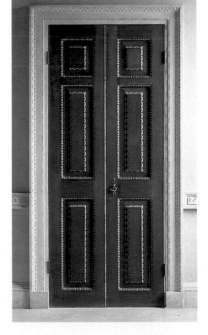

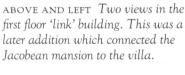

ABOVE AND LEFT *Two views in the first floor 'link' building. This was a later addition which connected the Jacobean mansion to the villa.*

OPPOSITE *The Blue Velvet Room that takes its name from the wallcovering. The ceiling, presumed to be the work of Kent, rests on heavy, richly ornamented console brackets. In the centre is an allegorical figure of Architecture crowned with a Corinthian capital and flanked by cherubs carrying drawing instruments.*

THE ROYAL AUTOMOBILE CLUB

THE ROYAL AUTOMOBILE CLUB began life in 1897 as a small social club at Whitehall Court (then at 119 Piccadilly). Its members were pioneers of the British motoring industry, and they decided to expand and build for themselves grand premises. In 1908 the present building in Pall Mall was started. It was finished in 1911 at the cost of £250,000.

Pall Mall is the heartland of London's senior clubs and the term Pall Mall is believed to come from the French *Paille Maille*, a ball game played by Charles II and friends in St James's Park.

The RAC building was designed by Charles Mewès and Arthur Davis. Mewès, a Frenchman, designed other buildings in London with Davis including the Ritz (see page 190). Davis himself, although born in London, studied extensively in Brussels and Paris and was a top student in the famous *Ecole des Beaux Arts*. Its general style is French Renaissance and the building is on the site of the old War Office. Indeed, in the smoke room of the Royal Automobile Club, there is an Adam ceiling from the old building.

The outside of the building is grand, even slightly numbing in its Imperial regularity, but inside it is a mini-palace of opulence and Edwardian hedonism. The Club is particularly famous for its Byzantine torch-lit swimming pool – Geroge Bernard Shaw was a regular user. The entrance prepares you fully for the luxury to come: you enter beneath an Ionic portico and into a high glamorous oval-shaped vestibule. Then comes the classical French romp.

The Royal Automobile Club, like the Ritz, is a symbol of luxury; perhaps questionable luxury as the spies Burgess and Maclean had a final lunch together here before making off.

ABOVE *The Doric columns of the swimming pool area are inlaid with coloured mosaic patterns – a contemporary critic said it had an air of Roman design under a Greek influence.*

LEFT *Detail of the mosaic patterns decorating the columns.*

OPPOSITE *The sumptuous pool – the width is 30 feet and the length 86 feet. There are black marble bands inlaid in the floor of the bath. As the RAC Journal says, 'Few interiors present so attractive a problem to the architect, owing to the delightful effects provided by the reflection in, and reflected light from, the surface of the water.'*

BILL STICKERS

ALONGSIDE THE collection of record ads and gig guides that get plastered on any available hoarding space in this city, the immortal words 'Bill Stickers Will Be Prosecuted' inevitably appear as an ineffective deterrent. Poor old Bill, why pick on him? And now it turns up as a restaurant in Greek Street in the heart of Soho and in the midst of a concatenation of good restaurants and drinking houses.

Slow but sure hardly fits Bill Stickers, which looks decidedly raunchier, more raucous and distinctly odder than most restaurants. In fact it looks like the cover of the funkier kind of rock records that were popular in the early 1970s.

The style of Bill Stickers is comparable with that of Club 2000 (see page 150) and is intended to constantly stimulate the eyes while being also 'clubby' – warm and cosy. In a sense it is a swinger's version of the private pub at the Architectural Press (see page 125). In its current manifestation the Bill Stickers restaurant was designed by Tony and Robert Newmark. The place is run by them and their sister Patricia.

An 'informed' guide to such an outlandish interior seems almost ludicrous, but there is something in its eclectism, in its whamming together of ethnic bits and pieces, in the overall approach of collage and assemblage, that says its roots are in the mainstream of modern art. The men who began this started 70 years ago – Picasso for one, Kurt Schwitters for another. They found things, tore things up, and stuck them into sculptures or walls or pictures. It is a phenomenon entirely understandable in the 20th century – there is just so much stuff that you hardly need to make any more but can simply reconfigure it endlessly.

ABOVE *The mask came from Tahiti and a quasi-Venetian balustrade was constructed around it. There are other voodoo masks around the building.*

LEFT *The bar by the front entrance has a zebra stripe decoration specially designed in Italy. The* wooden panelling, the deep crimson and the heavy curtains are intended to create an entrance of welcome.

OPPOSITE *The chandelier, it is claimed, came originally from the Palace of Versailles. The figure is a representation of Robert Newmark as a devil.*

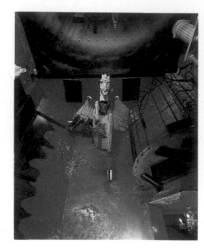

ABOVE *Pegasus, seen by the owners as a symbol of hope, made in plaster and embellished with ostrich feathers and glass jewellery.*

RIGHT *The ceiling painted in the dome is an upside-down view of Manhattan Island, New York. It took three months to paint.*

THE RED HOUSE

Two things make this house fascinating: first, its impact on Victorian design was startling; second, it was commissioned by William Morris, one of Britain's most influential theorists and craftsmen. The architect was Philip Webb.

William Morris is most widely known for his wallpapers and his textile designs – he had a genius for pattern and for two-dimensional design. He was also a designer of furniture. Equally important for contemporary historians and politicians is Morris's career as a moralist and socialist polemicist. He was highly critical of the un-aesthetic, unethical and downright cruel conditions of Victorian industry. What Morris did was focus modern attention on the awful effects that uncontrolled industrialisation was having on the fabric of the cities and the countryside and the daily lives of men, women and children.

Morris was not, of course, the only sensitive Victorian. Other Victorians campaigned and fortunately succeeded in improving the country's infrastructure. The provision of clean drinking water, the introduction of sewers, the foundations of a state education system were all significant, but what Morris rightly stressed was the importance of art and, most important of all, the fundamental need to make work as pleasurable and as creative as possible.

The work done in the Victorian factories and on Victorian farms was painful – the working day was very long, poorly paid and the homes, nutrition and healthcare enjoyed by the workforce was primitive indeed. Work was thus perpetual drudgery, it was a continuous pain.

Morris believed that a return to the idea of the craftsman was essential – it was to be a return to the type of work whereby a man or woman worked at making an object and did so with freedom of will – working at one's own pace, not that of a machine and working on the whole thing, and not just one part of it. Morris looked back to the medieval years when, he assumed, more people were happy in their work. He did not reject the machine but did not want the machine to supplant the creative aspects of work.

His view of the past was undoubtedly over-rosy and he seemed to make the mistake which John Ruskin, his mentor, had warned against, which was not to assume that just because a beautiful handmade object gives you pleasure that it had also given its maker pleasure. Nevertheless, in drawing attention to the ideal that work should not be dominated by monotony and

ABOVE *Many people close to William Morris contributed to the decoration including Edward Burne-Jones and Dante Gabriel Rossetti.*

LEFT *A stylistic feature of the house is a three-tier rhythm to the design and decoration – these windows show it well. We step down from rectangle to circle to a delicate pattern of trefoils.*

OVERLEAF *Webb invented a new English vernacular, part Gothic and part rural barn.*

that there should be freedom for expression, Morris contributed to a revolution in education and in the social theory of work thinking that has not diminished.

Morris and his new wife Jane (Burden) moved into the Red House in 1860. It is a remarkable building because its cleanliness and lack of clutter, its emphasis upon space and light recalls the spirit (but not the forms) of 18th-century classicism. It renounces Victorian materialism and introduces an English vernacular. It is a statement of puritanism and clarity. Yet its puritanism should not be confused with utilitarianism, for it is essentially romantic. Rossetti wrote of it as a 'most noble work in every way, and more a poem than a house.' Its very name describes it without ambiguity; its brilliant red brick, when new and before English weather had mellowed it, and its orange-red tile roof – long before Norman Shaw used them to such effect – were startlingly novel.

LEFT *We see how well things fit together to make homely still-lifes – the Medieval architecture of the dresser, like the front of a large building, is a perfect foil for objects with fussier and more detailed surfaces. The dresser and the fabric designs are by Morris.*

ABOVE *The inside of the main door is a tour de force, an absolutely brilliant composition in formal decoration, creatively set off by the William Morris wallpaper.*

BRIAN JUHOS' HOUSE

ONE OF THE FASCINATING aspects of London is the change that has befallen many of the houses. A great deal of the elegant Victorian stucco houses that border the squares of Bayswater and Westbourne Grove have seen their status as individual homes ravaged by landlords in the 1950s and 1960s dividing spacious rooms up into 'bedsits'. The estate agents' jargon for such property now is the euphemistic understatement known as 'studio'. Throughout the 1970s and 1980s, building-boom developers carved these magnificent buildings into even more individual units, squeezing out the last drop of living space.

These became 'stunning', 'luxurious', 'spacious' or 'magnificent' – descriptions that in any other business would be prosecuted under the trade descriptions act. Because of this misuse of language, to say nothing of the misuse of property, it is difficult to find the words that will convincingly describe an apartment that is truly all of these without diminishing the skill and imagination of the interior designer whose home we see here.

Brian Juhos has succeeded in creating a home for himself out of a near-vandalised set of rooms that to any developer would surely have made at least three flats. To be fair, it could be said

ABOVE *A detailed arrangement in Brian's apartment clearly illustrates his passion for collecting. The juxtaposition of such objects highlights the care he lavishes on areas even away from the main line of vision.*

FAR LEFT *The entrance hall is visually deceptive. Its spaciousness is created by a full-length wall mirror.*

LEFT *The dining room with its two full-length windows that lead on to a balcony. On the left is a large glazed bookcase. Even this is unable to accommodate an ever-growing collection of books.*

OPPOSITE *The living room in its candlelit splendour.*

that it *was* two flats as the apartment has been converted laterally from the first floor of two adjoining houses.

Walking up the communal staircase from the ground floor there is little to indicate to the first-time visitor what is in store. But once in Brian's hallway one is left in no doubt that here lives somebody who passionately cares not only about his immediate surroundings but about the nature of buildings in general. Mirrors and statues create a feeling of spaciousness more in keeping with a large rambling town house than a flat.

Brian has taken full advantage of the ceiling heights and has cleverly created more space by giving the illusion that there is another floor. This can be seen by the staircase leading from the vestibule, just off the living room, to the guest bathroom. This in

fact is over his own en-suite bathroom and both are accommodated in the original height of a rear room.

The living room, lit at night almost entirely by candles, is the original size. Three elegant floor-to-ceiling windows extend along one wall. These in turn open on to a balcony overlooking the tree-laden square. The high ceilings and intricate cornices have been retained or renovated, as have the panelled doors and flooring. The room has been filled with paintings and furniture collected over the years or given as gifts by friends. This eclecticism has blended together to form an intimate and reassuring environment. Creating a home is an act of will acting on a series of guesses and choices. Even the acceptance of gift is a creative choice.

LITTLE HOLLAND HOUSE

LITTLE HOLLAND HOUSE was built by hand between 1902-4 by Frank Dickinson and his brothers, with the help of a brick-layer and a labourer. Dickinson also made the furniture and designed the silverware which he gave to his wife as a Silver Wedding present. He was a compulsive producer of things – fireplace surrounds, door plates, fire screens, rugs, bowls, lamps, coat racks and curtains. The domestic landscape became his work of art. He took his cue from John Ruskin:

'We will make some small piece of English land beautiful, peaceful and fruitful.'

Was Dickinson then a rich man? No, he was an idealist, a product of John Ruskin and of William Morris, a man who held to the Morris ideal that one should have *nothing* in one's home that one did not know to be either beautiful or useful. He was a radical but clearly not a bloody revolutionary. His work, his house, his optimism is enormously encouraging – it is a positive

ABOVE *The fireplace of the living room with an elaborately painted triptych depicting Good Husbandry – but the work is tongue-in-cheek.*

ABOVE *The walnut firescreen in William Morris style. This fireplace is in the dining room; the coal scuttle on the right was made by Dickinson.*

TOP *The panel above the living room fireplace is a scene in moulded plaster of dancing nymphs and piping boys – Pan-like but lacking the usual goat legs and ears. This is pastiche, a private joke.*

ABOVE *The panel above the fireplace in the dining room is in beaten copper – Dickinson turned his hand to all materials. As he went on through his house his skill in decorative composition grew.*

ABOVE *The bedstead was made and carved by Dickinson. The inscription reads 'O sleep it is a gentle thing'. The painting above is a picture of Morpheus or Somnus or Hypnos, classical Gods of Sleep.*

OPPOSITE *The living room showing the carved walnut chairs of which Dickinson was proud. He wrote, 'Even Chippendale would say, "Well done amateur craftsman".'*

rebuke to the nihilism of so much of today's art and design.

Little Holland House, 40 Beeches Avenue, Carshalton is described in the locally-produced guide as 'a complete record of a working man's life that is without parallel in these islands, as well as a testament to the Arts and Crafts Movement.' Dickinson was multi-talented – a painter, poet, woodcarver and metalsmith, he earned his living from such occupations as working for the Royal Doulton company.

The emphasis upon individuality and on doing everything himself is partly a result of economic necessity but also a testimony to his delight in freely engaging in work by choice. Freed from the burden to make one's handicraft economic and competitive one can lavish 'uneconomic time' upon it and turn out something really beautiful.

The account in the local guide book, (the house is happily well looked after by the London Borough of Sutton) of how Dickinson began preparing for his marriage is touching: 'he started making his furniture some three years before his marriage. At night in the cellar of his parent's house, he began to saw up by hand the enormous planks of walnut and pine he had bought. Helped by Florence [his future wife] he made the coal-box, then the dining table, bedstead and dressing table...'

THE WATER TOWER APARTMENT

THE VICTORIANS BEQUEATHED us many large buildings and these are enthusiastically recycled by people who want the thickening of age and texture that only an old building can provide. This is not simple backward lookingness: stone, wood and brick very often do look better after they have weathered. Perhaps we like the sense of continuity. Whatever the reason, it is very difficult to age entire buildings artificially and people are unprepared to wait.

This Victorian water tower is at the New Concordia Wharf. Once it formed part of a complex of industrial warehouses; these have been converted into flats or offices. Compared with the majority of new residential dwellings in the docklands – which are silly, Noddyland buildings for people with no visual discrimination but good credit ratings – the old big brick buildings have dignity and, moreover, lots of space.

The architect Piers Gough has converted this water tower building into a home. The tower is nine storeys high and the apartment occupies the top five floors. It is interesting that it is the Art Deco, or rather the 1930s, element that perhaps dominates the atmosphere of the apartment. In fact, despite the huge professional and critical debate about the style of the 1980s – *post-modernism* – what the style of the 1980s really reflects is the 1930s. It is Art Deco reinvented. This is true of the 'Roman Doric' pillars used throughout the house. They look suitable for a cinema. They are, in fact, radiators.

Overall the interior is exciting because the different levels have been exploited so that one has odd views into and across rooms – it is as if one of those wretchedly complicated three-dimensional wooden puzzles had been partially hollowed out and you are inside, wandering about.

The play-off between brick, wood and metal is a pleasure throughout and the owners have used such decorative touches as curtains and rugs to very nice, very precise effect. The cleanness of the wood finishes and the use of large areas of smooth unfussy plaster work provides a refreshing green salad to the meat of the walls.

One thing is striking: the quality of the workmanship. Good architects and good buildings need good clients who have patience to see a thing through – and workmanship of this standard, though clearly not intricate in the fashion of a Robert Adam interior, takes time. The old shell provides instant atmosphere; the contents are the result of deferred gratification.

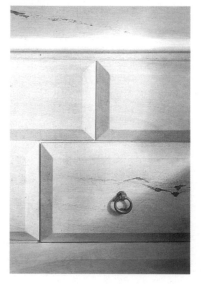

ABOVE *The entrance hall is clever; it seems to capitalise on asymmetry and yet the parts fit and balance like a well-proportioned face. The trick is in the angled hand rail.*

LEFT *Detail of the kitchen units.*

OPPOSITE *The kitchen does not impinge at all and the effect of a 'ruined temple' is deliberate. The pillars are radiators, painted black; they are flat-fronted panels turned back to front to show the ribbing.*

ABOVE LEFT *Piers Gough has used the textures of structures without indulging himself in a round of brutalism – you can imagine that, in the late 1960s (fire regulations permitting) the desire would have been to expose the beams in all their bluntness. The brackets are somewhat curious.*

LEFT *These windows (12 in all) were specially created by Gough and they are hung with twill sheeted curtain material. The finesse of Gough's work is apparent in the way everything fits – the radiators here, for example, flower gracefully into the detailing of brick headers around the arches.*

ABOVE *The games room. The venetian blinds used throughout are wooden, the lighting is tungsten halogen. All-natural materials surround the full-size billiards table, giving the room a raw, instantly aged but friendly atmosphere.*

Gough, the designer, is a partner in the practice of Cambell Zogolovitch Wilkinson and Gough. CZWG have been involved in the refurbishment or building of many properties within the docklands, perhaps the most controversial of which has been Cascades on the Isle of Dogs. This has been described as looking like a ski slope or an ocean liner, and has come in for special criticism from the Prince of Wales.

THE FREEMASONS' HALL

THE FREEMASONS' HALL was greeted enthusiastically by many architectural modernists – pleased that its construction signalled the sweeping away of the remnants of squalor and poverty that characterised the area.

The Freemasons' Hall was built in 1927–33 as the ceremonial and administrative headquarters for the United Grand Lodge of England. Designed by H.V. Ashley and F. Winton Newman, it was first known as the Masonic Peace Memorial and honoured the English Freemasons killed in the First World War.

The shape of the Freemasons' Hall is that of an irregular hollow pentagon, and the ceremonial entrance is marked by a classical tower. The pivot of the building is the Grand Temple which is really a great meeting hall.

The use of terms such as the 'Grand Temple' is confusing for those of us who are not masons, moreover it makes people suspicious about the rites and beliefs of the masons. What on earth do they do in there? Freemasonry is not a religion; the Freemasons do not allow religion to be discussed at their meetings, but what they ask of their members is a belief in a 'supreme being', and there are certainly rites and rituals. As the masons' official literature says, the members are taught the moral precepts of the organisation through ritual dramas using 'ancient forms, stonemasons' customs and tools as allegorical guides'.

So for the student of symbolic architecture this is interesting because in its planning, decoration and furnishings, the designs make use of a shared vocabulary of form and meaning. The richness of the ornament generated through the Freemasons can be enjoyed in the museum on the first floor.

ABOVE AND LEFT *The mosaic and marble floor decoration of the third vestibule (ante-chamber to the Grand Temple), with a central multi-pointed star inlaid with the semi-precious stone lapis lazuli.*

OVERLEAF *The outer face of the Grand Temple doors. These are bronze, with each door weighing one and a quarter tons. The top panels depict the procession of dedication of the Temple, the remaining six show scenes of the building of King Solomon's Temple.*

Guided tours of the building are available and it is in the ceremonial suite that the outsider begins to comprehend the sweep and complexity of the ritual that is the fabric of Freemasonry. The head of the Grand Lodge of England is called, appropriately enough, the Grand Master. He has a small suite for himself and his entourage to assemble in before proceeding along the Processional Corridor. At either end of the corridor there are stained glass windows depicting the four cardinal virtues of Justice, Prudence, Temperance and Fortitude, together with Charity. The procession then moves through three vesti-bules, each of increasing architectural richness, and climaxes in the Grand Temple itself.

As one of the world's oldest secular fraternal societies whose internal affairs are secret, the Freemasons have attracted comment and speculation. The secrecy is understandable because it allows members to relax in the confidence that nothing they say or do will be betrayed. Loyalty is an attractive commodity in the workaday civilian world. Much of the Freemasons' work is in fact charitable and using Freemasonry to promote self-interest is condemned.

ABOVE *The Memorial window and shrine which is in the first vestibule and is in memory of the English Freemasons who died during the First World War.*

LEFT *The Grand Temple looking towards the Grand Master's throne and pedestal. Above is a part of the deeply coffered ceiling – showing Jacob's ladder with King Solomon on the left, and King Hiram on the right.*

THE TOWER HOUSE

ONE'S 20TH-CENTURY MIND and eyes are too easily blunted by the possession of a narrow view of progress and modernity. We seem often to need things that look new in order to accept them as our own rather than as belonging to our forefathers. But there is no rational basis for this demand.

The Victorian philosopher and architectural critic John Ruskin said, 'We want no new style of architecture but we want some style.' He argued in particular for Gothic style.

By the mid-19th century Neo-Gothic had become the prevalent style although it was not used very much in domestic or business architecture. The most influential designers in Gothic were A.W.N. Pugin (see page 113) and William Butterfield (see page 184). Ruskin acted as the guardian of aesthetic and moral integrity (with books such as *The Seven Lamps of Architecture*). He promoted Gothic national style and saved it from being too narrowly associated with Anglo-Catholicism. Ruskin's advocacy of Italian Gothic, together with Butterfield's startling All Saints' Church, (in all its polychromatic glory) infused Neo-Gothic with splendour – and permanent colour. Architects became encouraged to build in the polychromy of richly veined marbles. Designers, such as William Burges (1827-1881), put intense colour and ornament into their furniture and furnishings.

In Ruskin's view Gothic was a *natural*, organic approach to building. But, looking back, it was also a materialistic style: there is much added value, much obvious wealth, much actual

ABOVE *The outer porch with mosaic wall and floor covering; out of sight is a mosaic of Burges' favourite dog 'Pinky'.*

RIGHT *The main entrance hall complete with fireplace and dog grate. The hall stretches upwards to the wooden gallery on the next floor.*

TOP RIGHT *The gallery overlooking the hall, with painted ceiling showing the constellations in the position they were in when the house was first used.*

FAR RIGHT *The decorated glass in the entrance hall depicts the four seasons. Shown here is winter.*

OPPOSITE *The dining room with Devonshire marble walls, a frieze of glazed tiles, and enamelled iron ceiling panels depicting the zodiac.*

and (therefore expensive) detailing. It is clamorous, at times almost nouveau riche.

And this is the home that William Burges had built for himself. An architect and designer, Burges was described in 1880 as either an architect working 50 years before his time or working on an entirely mistaken track.

An expert on 13th-century Gothic, Burges was also deeply interested in Japanese art. What he admired was delicacy, good craftsmanship and decoration that had an easily inferred content. He loved colour and invested his interiors with hues of Babylonian intensity.

His designs were not commercially produced but commissioned by individual patrons. Skilled craftsmen were used and the designs were executed with exceptional flair. There are examples of Burges' design work in the Victoria & Albert Museum including a large, richly carved and gilded wooden bed with a headboard painted with *The Judgement of Paris*.

TOP LEFT *The library looking through to the music room.*

LEFT *The fireplace in the library, one of Burges's most ambitious undertakings. The chimney-piece is a Medieval castle, which is also the Tower of Babel – the figures represent the dispersal of the parts of speech. (The whole house in fact is based, lightheadtedly, on the idea of a castle.) The alphabet letters are in Caen stone, the plain surround is Mexican onyx.*

ABOVE LEFT *A detail from one of the doors of the elaborately painted bookcases in the library. These were the work of Fred Weekes, and depict an occupation for each separate letter of the alphabet, such as M for Mason. On the inside of each door is a small intricate painting of a bird. These were executed by H. Stacey Marks.*

ABOVE RIGHT *Detail of frieze with fish and eels in the sea, in Burges's own bedroom.*

The interior of the Tower House unfolds in a series of fantasy narratives. When you enter through the entrance hall you see black griffins on guard at the large grey stone fireplace. On the mosaic floor Theseus is caught in the slaying of a minotaur. Above each of the entrances to the rooms there is a symbol representing the function of that particular room.

The Library is interesting for its painted cupboards and each of these represents a different letter of the alphabet (A–V) and each portrays a man involved in an activity – A = Astronomer, B = Bricklayer, P = Painter, Q = Quarry Worker. The inside of each cupboard is embellished with a small square painting of the head of a bird in the centre of each door. Beneath each cupboard are painted drawers.

The windows are painted with pictorial representations of various disciplines from the arts and sciences such as poetry, astronomy, and literature. The fireplace is decorated with a Medieval caste and figures and each is labelled with definitions of the parts of speech – noun, preposition, verb and so forth.

It is a little as if Gradgrind had taken to decoration as a pedagogic art, for the same literalness, the emphasis upon word and object, continues in the other rooms. In the dining room for instance, there are signs of the zodiac painted on the ceiling. The windows, appropriately enough, carry figures who are serving fish, wine, fowl, meat and vegetables. There is a frieze showing scenes from fairy tales and folk stories including Babes in the Wood, Robin Hood, and Little Red Riding Hood.

Much of the house is directed towards the upbringing of young children and to giving them a basic education. And, in a heavy handed way, it does set out to entertain but sadly there were no children to complete the logic of the enterprise, although upstairs there are two children's bedrooms. One of these has Jack and the Beanstalk adorning the fireplace and a truly horrid giant emerges egregiously from the chimney-piece. The tower, around which the house is built, suggests a fairy story.

ABOVE *One of the panels in the music room. The overall theme of the music room is 'tender passion of love' – which music feeds.*

ABOVE *Themed decoration is carried out in all the details. These brass-plated light switches represent (on the left) the library and (on the right) the music room.*

RIGHT *Looking from the music room through to the library.*

THE HALLS' HOUSE

Do THE AVANT GARDE understand this kind of interior? It is not ironic, it makes use of 'history' but for pleasure, not polemics and it is the kind of interior you feel comfortable in. You can sit on a chair in the expectation that it will not assault you with its angularity. No, that's nonsense – you sit down in one of Jenny Hall's interiors without any thoughts about awkwardness at all.

This house fulfils many desirable criteria: it is interesting, and is filled with a variety of colour, textures, sound and light. It is an agreeable mixture of old and new; it is a shade Hiltonesque but that's because the major rich hoteliers do insist on making their institutions domestic in an upmarket sort of way.

Naturally this house has been featured in *The World of Interiors* – a magazine equivalent of a coming-out ball for interior designers. Jenny Hall is not an interior designer, it is just that over the years she has been through nineteen houses and redecorated the lot. This house in Kensington is her twentieth. (Jenny Hall is married to a banker.)

She told *The World of Interiors* that each house has to have a starting point – and here the decor has been unravelled from a stone arch which she bought, in pieces, in Siena. Sienese is the flavour of the house. It is a predilection for the dustiness, the chalkiness, the intense yet oddly fugitive colours of the fresco. The other texture prominent in the house is terracotta: thus the catalyst textures are marble, chalk, and clay.

This is a nostalgic interior – it is not a replication of a new Siena but an old one. In this it is very English. The dominant style in Englishness is weathered, soiled, used, old. Hence the fact that the terracotta tiles (which were new) had to be aged by the builder and his mates who stamped dirt and linseed oil into them. One wonders what the builder's mates thought.

ABOVE RIGHT *Dry earthy colours dominate; the walls are plain to set off the areas of concentrated ornamentation. The paint on the walls was applied with a sponge. The chandelier is Venetian.*

RIGHT *The drawing room with sponged stone coloured walls; in the centre is a banquette. The parquet flooring is new, and waxed and polished each week.*

OPPOSITE *Another view of the drawing room; the wing chair is tapestry-covered and its scumbled, textile surface picks up the faded, fugitive effect that gives this house its atmosphere.*

Jenny Hall's word is *soul*. That is what she seeks. Clearly an eclectic, she alights on things in her travels and develops a passion for them. She went to Egypt and tried to buy a house in Luxor – but could not, so is now creating an Egyptian house out of their home in Spain.

She clearly has a talent for colour and her handling in this house of the rich reds, ochres and greens is strongly reminiscent of the William Burges house (see page 172). The ability to handle this intensity of colour is quite rare, partly because it has been knocked out of interior design tradition – now there are usually the discreet formal pastels of classicism or the greys and whites of modernists.

LEFT *A view down to the first floor landing.*

BELOW *A corner in the main bedroom which emphasises Jenny Hall's attention to detail. Above the marble fireplace is a painting by Wiefeld,* Breton Women. *In the corner is an arrangement of dogwood. The room reflects the feeling of the ensuing season that can be seen beyond the window.*

THE WREN CHAPEL

THE GRACEFUL CHANGES that Wren wrought to the skylines of London remained unchallenged until the 1960s. What happened subsequently is history. Sir Christopher Wren (1632-1723) built on the work of Inigo Jones in that he developed and spread English Classicism. But gradually he became involved with the Baroque (a heavily ornamental style) and the Royal Naval College, Greenwich, formerly the Naval Hospital, is Wren's Baroque masterpiece.

Greenwich is a fabulous sight: it is best seen from across the river looking south from the Isle of Dogs, and if you frame your eyes so that you block out the power stations and industrial junk on either side, you have the very essence of civilised harmony and architectural drama.

The association between Greenwich and the Royal Navy began under the Tudors. Henry VIII was born at Greenwich and he established the naval dockyards at Deptford and Woolwich. In 1694, William and Mary, King and Queen of England, granted permission for a Hospital for Seamen to be built on the site of Charles I's Greenwich Palace – this was little more than a shell, there having been insufficient money to complete it. In fact the building had already been used to house the wounded of the Battle of La Hogue in 1692; its conversion and extension was a form of gratitude and offering for the Anglo-Dutch victory over the French. Wren, with Thomas Ripley, designed the Chapel of St Peter and St Paul for the Hospital; it was completed 20 years after Wren's death. However, 75 years after its completion its interior was ravaged by fire and what we see here today is in fact the work of another architect, James Stuart.

Wren's Chapel is a grandly generous space which can accommodate 1,500 people. The interior was remodelled by James

ABOVE *The black and white marble floor is inset in the central aisle with the emblem, in gold, of the Seamen's Hospital.*

LEFT *The incredible ornate plasterwork of the ceiling.*

OVERLEAF *The shell-shaped niches on either side of the columns flanking the altar are typical of 18th-century classicism. The altar painting is by Benjamin West and illustrates Acts 27 and 28.*

Stuart in the neo-Greek style between 1779 and 1788. James 'Athenian' Stuart (1713-88) was a fan painter before visiting Rome. With his collaborator, the architect Nicholas Revett, he gained support from the Society of Dilettanti in London to spend 1751-53 in Greece to make drawings and views of Athenian buildings. Stuart then began urging the case that Greek architecture was superior to Roman.

Stuart, regarded by architectural historians as a major architect whose promise was diluted by laziness, completed another major work (Mrs Montagu's house) in Portman Square (c.1775) but this was destroyed in the Second World War. The Greenwich Hospital Chapel is his finest surviving work.

Stuart and Revett published a series of volumes of drawings, the *Antiquities of Athens*. These drawings revealed the strength and simplicity of the Greek doric order of pillar; the Greek doric is shorter and thicker than the Roman, with no base. Any change in any architectural orthodoxy causes arguments and this Greek version caused a considerable row among the Palladians (the classical old guard). But the Greek doric order became the *leitmotif* of the Greek Revival Style.

The vestibule of the Chapel, on the north front, is entered through a portico and a large rectangular entry. The exterior pattern of niches and panels continues inside the Chapel, and the theme is picked up by the composition of round-headed windows on the east and west sides. One of the features of the decoration are the *Grisaille* panels (a French technique of monochrome painting in shades of grey, which imitate the effect of relief). These panels depict saints and biblical characters and they punctuate the rhythm of windows.

The shallow vaulted roof is decorated with plaster work in the Grecian style, principally in a pattern of rosettes and scroll work based on Greek vases. The blue, cream and dull yellow colour scheme belongs to the Greek style and was used by Josiah Wedgwood for his Etruscan Ware ceramics.

LEFT *The gold lectern is richly carved with maritime symbolism. The organ carries on the visual harmony. Within the classical, geometric sequence, the decoration is relatively restrained. The Grisaille panels are visible, left and right on the east and west walls.*

ABOVE *Looking upwards to the height of the organ. The sequence of the frieze, borders and decorated plaster panels (bordered with a Greek key pattern) carries through above the carved wooden pinnacles of its gold-coloured pipes.*

DEBENHAM HOUSE

FILM MAKERS LIKE to use this exotic romp of an interior for their more sensational scenes. Built in 1905-07, it was designed by Halsey Ricardo. Ricardo was a prominent member of the Art Workers' Guild, itself a child of the Century Guild. Ricardo was committed to restoring building, crafts and decorative arts to their rightful place beside painting and sculpture.

Externally, with its glazed tiles and Staffordshire bricks, this building was a serious attempt to resist pollution. The *Architectural Review* in 1907 said, 'the city dirt has only a precarious lodgement on the glazed surfaces, so that both wind and rain help to keep the house clean, and the rain falls as swiftly off the building as it does off a garden.'

The interior was a collaboration between Ricardo and Arts and Crafts practitioners. Perhaps the most important influence internally on this house, which was commissioned by Sir Ernest Debenham, was William de Morgan. He had wanted to be a painter but changed to designing in the applied arts instead. He worked for a while with William Morris and set up his own pottery in 1869. His speciality was tiles and he revived the craft of lustre (the surface of lustre ware is iridescent and metallic), and his favoured colours were the Persian hues – green, black and turquoise. A favourite de Morgan motif, appropriately, is the peacock.

Symbolism in the architecture is present in the library, where the mahogany bookcase shelves are inlaid in ivory and mother of pearl in the form of moths, lilies and pansies. The pansies illustrate the double meaning of the French word *pensée* – pansy and thought. The moths symbolise evening hours, and their small winged ivory hour-glasses symbolise the flight of time.

ABOVE *William de Morgan tiles from the Fulham pottery.*

ABOVE *Even the door furniture is exquisite – brass, cut and embossed with enamel in the shape of butterflies and leaves.*

FAR LEFT *Main entrance door in mahogany topped with a carved frieze of dragons, the whole set off by the blue and grey veined marble, worked and cut to Halsey Ricardo's designs.*

OPPOSITE *The hall. The mosaic depicts entertaining bloody scenes from Greek myths – the Argonauts challenging Scylla, Jason retrieving the Golden Fleece. There are also profiles of the Debenham family and the signs of the zodiac.*

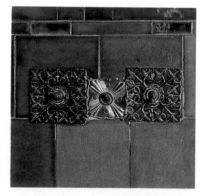

ABOVE *New technology tamed and made pretty – as these elaborate brass electric light switches show.*

ALL SAINTS' CHURCH

GOTHIC ARCHITECTURE of the Victorian era is loathed by the modernists and those who build in the style deplored by the Prince of Wales; this is unsurprising given that one generation rejects the work of its parents, can tolerate the work of its grandparents but really loves that of its great grandparents. Yet Victorian Gothic in all its phases stayed out of favour longer than most – or did it? Is it not perhaps possible that in the eyes and minds of ordinary, intelligent laypeople an affection continued for the style?

Whatever the truth, architects such as William Butterfield are happily favoured again, and their interiors are no longer painted over or hidden in disgrace behind modern coverings.

Butterfield (1814-1900) was a passionate man, an architect who worked in a decorated form of high Victorian Gothic, and a man whose virtues have been trumpeted by an equally passionate man, the contemporary critic Peter Fuller. His description of the interior of All Saints', in Margaret Street is vivid: 'Through its extraordinary ornamental system, a wide range of geological and man-made materials were organised into brash and unprecedented abstract patterns. All these stones and techniques seem about to burst forth from the Gothic constraints, which nonetheless contain them. Butterfield forced and twisted his structural forms so that his magnificent building rises like a resplendent pheasant around the compressed perimeter of the tiny quadrangle in which it is placed.'

Butterfield built All Saints' Church to replace the decaying Margaret Chapel for its congregation and for the Cambridge Camden Society, a reforming Anglican High Church movement. Butterfield had a passion which he wanted his buildings to express, and he had a vocabulary of form and symbolism by which that passion could be shared.

Many critics are concerned about the apparent emptiness in art and architecture today: the pressing question is, what can artists and architects do and make which will have meaning in an age which has very few shared beliefs? Because, while the majority of people still believe in 'something', this 'something' is vague and inconclusive. It is good that our attention has been drawn to an architect whose own age – the mid-19th century – was no less riven by doubt than our own. Fuller says of Butterfield's work that it was 'the struggle to maintain an imaginative and spiritual relationship with the "natural creation" at a time of dawning realisation that this creation did not reveal God.'

ABOVE *Butterfield had wanted a full chancel screen, but the founders insisted that the altar, font, and pulpit be visible anywhere in the Church. The foliage designs in alabaster granite are reflected elsewhere in the building.*

RIGHT *The decoration of the pulpit (multi-coloured inlaid marble on granite columns) echoes that of the church generally. Butterfield sought unified ornamentation.*

OPPOSITE, ABOVE *The original Jesse window designed by Alfrede Gerente was disliked because of its general cabbage green and yellow colour. Alexander Gibbs produced a replacement in 1877 under the direction of William Butterfield.*

OPPOSITE, BELOW *The Sanctuary has been cleaned recently. William Dyce painted the frescos on the east wall but these disintegrated and after a botched restoration the frescos were covered up with panels painted by Ninian Comper in 1909.*

THE WARRINGTON HOTEL

THE WARRINGTON HOTEL is a fine example of an Edwardian bar, beautifully kept up and a living rebuke to those landlords and breweries who are turning good bars and public houses into romper rooms for the trendy young. Nothing that the new designers are doing to pubs will last; this is not said from sentimentality for the old, but merely as a reflection on the times. Interior design now, as opposed to then, is done on the assumption that it will be ripped out and replaced every five years.

Pubs and bars are now corralled into a thing called the *leisure industry*. The high priests of this industry assume that decors have to keep changing to 'attract the younger punters'. They will ignore an ageing population at their peril. Who over 30 wants to drink as part of a leisure industry? Who wants to sit in decor thought up by a marketing executive with a head full of Croydonesque marketing speak?

The pub, that enclosing, fuggy crimson and flocked womb, has nurtured many a male writer. One of the best novels to be written for years was Kingsley Amis's Booker Prize-winning *The Old Devils*, and pubs and pub conversation provided the book's physical landscape.

Edwardian bars have much about them that is comforting but some of them are a bit rheumy-eyed, a bit too close to the oppressive old 'Bull 'n Bush' matiness of a Saturday night in working class London. This, the Warrington Hotel, is a little bit of posh. It has a touch of class that provides a perfect backdrop for those nicer Alan Bennett characters to meet, to court or to gossip.

So the Warrington gets a better class of customer, always did. That is what the decoration is there for, that is why the room, although large, is so domestic in its fiddly bits, so fussy with its crushed velour-topped stools and its fancy floral carpet.

The dominant style in this bar is probably best described as Art Nouveau – those swirling figures painted above the bar exhibit all the Art Nouveau tendencies: attentuated forms, curving, flowing lines, lots of long rippling hair and a flavour of decadence. The style peaked around about 1900 but continued until the beginning of the First World War.

What is especially intriguing about this bar is its altar-like arrangement; this is drinking in the round and doing so in some glory beneath a canopy held up by a pair of ripe cherub-like aquatic boys provoking a mood of alcoholic reverie.

ABOVE *In this view of the bar the Art Nouveau figures are plain to see and so too are the delightful brass shell light fittings. The jelly mould glass light shades are another nice touch.*

LEFT *The fruity putti finish off the wave motif very stylishly but by the end of an evening so much swirling makes the eyes roll.*

BELOW LEFT *Red was a favourite Edwardian colour although here it kills off the little touches of Primavera-style garlanding. Between the arches is more Art Nouveau decoration but these figures are rather crude in their drawing.*

OPPOSITE *The full glory of the bar with its rich mahogany base and marble top. Note too the elaborate glasswork right and left.*

THE GREEK CATHEDRAL

THE CONVERSION OF THE NATIVES in Britain to Christianity took several hundred years and the persistent effort of a variety of foreign missionaries. Greek missionaries visited England in the 2nd century AD and continued for centuries after. Many of the visitors were academics and they had a profound effect on moulding English thought and English culture. In fact, in AD 669 Theodore of Tarsus became Archbishop of Canterbury.

Naturally, as England edged its way through the Medieval centuries and into a unified trading and manufacturing entity, the men from Greece and Asia Minor who owned ships, and traded in textiles, spices and metal wares, found it convenient to settle in the City of London.

The first Greek Church was opened in 1677. The Bishop of London, Henry Compton, had been instrumental in obtaining special permission for this. The church was built between Greek Street and Charing Cross, and Soho street names such as Old Compton Street and Greek Street are reminders of the longevity of the relationship with the Greek community.

In 1872 the fathers of the Greek community decided that a new church was needed, one that was closer to where those of the Greek Orthodox faith were now living; a Building Committee was established and a lawyer and scholar called Edwin Freshfield played a leading role, both as a legal administrator and as Byzantinist. The architect, John Oldrid Scott, understood his patrons' wishes and created a building that firmly echoes the

ABOVE *The great golden dome and Pantokrator (Almighty God) who is ringed at the rim by the apostles and evangelists and an inner frieze of cherubim and seraphim.*

FAR LEFT *Mosaic floor beneath the dome. The double-headed eagle is an emblem of Eastern imperial power – it is placed so that it shows it is subject to the superior authority of God above.*

LEFT *The altar.*

OPPOSITE *The double Greek Cross hung with ruby lamps is suspended from the arch over the centre aisle.*

marvellous church of St Sophia in Constantinople. The site is unimpressive but the church is designated a Cathedral.

The interior is wondrous but it was not accomplished in one go. What we see today is a mature building; it has been served by a hundred years of devotion. It is a living alternative to the approach adopted by new churches of the 1960s (the Anglican cathedral in Coventry, for example) where an 'instant' decoration was cooked up to rather dismal effect. Of course, the art and decoration here had not sought to be avant garde, or par-

ticularly contemporary. It kept faith with its roots by using authentic designs wrought in the best materials, although scholars point out that this overly naturalistic representation of God and his apostles dilutes the Byzantine emphasis that 'roundness and perspective denote perfection'. One wonders if this matters over-much, bearing in mind that the context for this Cathedral is Western and therefore some influence of the host culture is both understandable and desirable. The Greek community is also British.

THE RITZ

EVERYONE IN LONDON has heard of the Ritz; it is *the* word in swankiness, a byword for class, style and wealth. The Ritz Hotel is named after a Swiss hotelier called Cesar Ritz who had drawn up the specifications; the architects were Mewès and Davis, also responsible for the Dorchester (see page 36).

The Ritz was the first major steel-framed building in London and opened in May 1906. It was also the first major building created by the Davis and Mewes partnership, although the main style was set by Davis. It is one of the most elegant buildings on Piccadilly and brings its style on to the street – the covered pavement arcade is French and is a close echo of the *Rue de Rivoli*. The French style is continued through the Classical design up to the mansard roofs. The outside walls are built from Norwegian granite and Portland stone.

Inside the hotel works up from luxury through to opulence. The scale of grandeur climbs as one enters the foyer and reception area past the grand staircase, past the elegant Edwardian Palm Court to the richly decorated restaurant. This columned restaurant overlooking Green Park is sumptuous. The Ritz is a fine example of the 19th-century Beaux Arts decoration.

The overall style is described as Louis XVI, with the decor and furnishings provided by Waring and Gillow. The whole scene has the rich lustre that only much-reflected light from good quality marble and genuine crystal chandeliers can create.

ABOVE *The focal point of the Palm Court is this fountain in which a steady jet of water springs up from the bowl. The lithe female statue is called 'La Source'.*

LEFT *The Palm Court.*

OPPOSITE *The restaurant overlooking Green Park with the trompe l'oeil sky ceiling and its frieze of Edwardian London.*

OVERLEAF *Possibly the most ostentatiously romantic setting in London.*

KEY TO EXTERIORS

ST PAUL'S CATHEDRAL
Ludgate
The City EC4

LEIGHTON HOUSE
Holland Park Road
Holland Park W14

THE 2000 CLUB
Wardour Street
Soho W1

CHISWICK HOUSE
Burlington Lane
Chiswick W4

THE ROYAL AUTOMOBILE CLUB
Pall Mall
St James's SW1

BILL STICKERS
Greek Street
Soho W1

THE RED HOUSE
Red House Lane
Bexleyheath DA6

BRIAN JUHOS' HOUSE
Cleveland Square
Bayswater W2

LITTLE HOLLAND HOUSE
Beeches Avenue
Carshalton SN5

THE WATER TOWER APARTMENT
New Concordia Wharf
Wapping SE1

THE FREEMASONS' HALL
Great Queen Street
Covent Garden WC2

THE TOWER HOUSE
Melbury Road
Holland Park W14

THE HALLS' HOUSE
Kensington Gate
Knightsbridge SW7

THE WREN CHAPEL
Royal Naval College
Greenwich SE10

DEBENHAM HOUSE
Addison Road
Holland Park W14

ALL SAINTS' CHURCH
Margaret Street
Marylebone W1

THE WARRINGTON HOTEL
Warrington Crescent
Maida Vale W9

THE GREEK CATHEDRAL
Moscow Road
Bayswater W2

THE RITZ
Piccadilly
St James's W1

CHAPTER FIVE

Into the 20th Century

Wᴇɴ ʜʀʜ ᴛʜᴇ ᴘʀɪɴᴄᴇ ᴏғ ᴡᴀʟᴇs entered the debate about modern architecture everyone except architects and architectural critics was amused. The public agreed with Charles. Twentieth-century architecture was a disappointment. In the age of the welfare state we had been given, not an architecture of public and democratic grandeur, but, especially in London, an age of grey concrete squalor. And it was not to do with a shortage of money – concrete is a very expensive way to build.

But, whatever our individual feelings about 'glass stumps' and whether or not architects have done more harm than the Luftwaffe, we would be misleading ourselves if we think of the 20th century only in terms of concrete and glass boxes. For the disenchantment is really with the period between the mid 1950s and the late 1970s. Both before and after there is a diversity of design and desire to entertain, to charm and to serve.

ᴏᴘᴘᴏsɪᴛᴇ *The atrium of the Cotton Centre at Hays Wharf, London docklands. In the late 1980s the scale, extent and financial vastness of the new building schemes in London has amazed some, appalled others. Public sculpture, which in Victorian times expressed with gravitas a range of civic values, now has a role as developer's bric-a-brac.*

ᴀʙᴏᴠᴇ *Detail from the Hoover Building. This was built between 1932-5. It is the classic 1930s factory, looking from the outside like an Art Deco palace. Its interiors were well done for the period – light, airy and warm; this modern factory sought to dignify labour.*

TV-AM STUDIOS

THE STUDIOS OF TV-AM, the breakfast-time television company, are in what is known as post-modernist style. Few architects are sure of what a handy definition of post-modernism should be except that, as a style, post-modernism should be decorative, witty, flamboyant and symbolic. In other words, it is different from the squared-off, plain-faced architecture of the modernism that pre-dates it.

In general a modern building of the late 1950s to late 1970s tends to be anonymous; a building after that date tends to strive for self-advertisement, or symbolism – a design that says something about what the occupants work at.

Terry Farrell, the architect who created the TV-am building out of an old garage in Camden, is Britain's leading post-modern architect. He is a friend and ally of Charles Jencks, the London-based American architect and author who coined the phrase 'post-modernism'. Farrell has worked on Jencks house in Holland Park (see page 198).

Breakfast television came late to Britain (1983) and TV-am, as a commercial rival to the BBC's own breakfast service, had a particularly difficult first year. But, and ironically after famous and glamorous media personalities like Anna Ford had left the company, TV-am revived, largely, it seems, through the unexpected popularity of the puppet character Roland the Rat. Industrial difficulties during 1988 made the company vulnerable again: such is the unpredictable nature of popular journalism.

The early financial difficulties have been blamed, in part, on lavish spending on the building. But lavish implies expensive and this building is not expensive; it is ostentatious, which is different.

The building had to be ostentatious because it is a piece of advertising as much as it is a piece of architecture. Like the Michelin building (see page 92) it is contributing to the company's function – making a profit from advertising. The main entrance is all Hollywood, while the view from Regent's Canal reveals a collection of giant breakfast eggs in fibreglass eggcups.

Inside the word is theatricality. Most of the materials and surfaces are faked up – what looks like stone is not, although some of the wood is solid. There are references to Mesopotamia, to Japan, and to the latest (early 1980s) in fashionable Italian design. The atrium, which was part of the original building, helps in the creation of a suitably large space so that a fulsome greeting for fulsome egos can be accommodated.

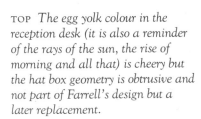

TOP *The egg yolk colour in the reception desk (it is also a reminder of the rays of the sun, the rise of morning and all that) is cheery but the hat box geometry is obtrusive and not part of Farrell's design but a later replacement.*

ABOVE LEFT AND RIGHT *Geometry abounds in this interior: the cylinder and the triangle are particularly*

dominant. It appears that Farrell has re-invented Art Deco, the design style of the 1930s, although within a tight budget.

OPPOSITE *The central axis of the building from the main entrance draws you to this 'Sunday Night At The London Palladium' sugar-candy staircase. It is an enticement to trip up and down.*

CHARLES JENCKS' HOUSE

EARLY IN THE 20th-century radical architects and critics campaigned against ornament. These 'modernists' designed buildings and furniture that were without decoration. They set their face against sculpture, carving, modelling and figurative ornament. New building techniques encouraged simple boxes – big boxes for offices and factories, little boxes for workers' houses. There was also a moral angle: rational, cleaned-up architecture, stripped bare of ornament, was a visual rebuff to bourgeois values. There were no sentimental sculptures, no decorated tiles, no *putti* or cherubs or naked Gods or vine leaves, or any of the other sentimental bric-a-brac favoured by merchants, bankers and middle class entrepreneurs.

After the Second World War the attractions of architecture without ornament and with big open spaces appealed strongly to the merchants and the bankers. By clearing away the clutter of embellishment you could build more quickly, more economically and design spaces that really were more utilitarian.

Modernism has not ruined the world, however. You can travel, for example, in France or Italy and not feel that the cities and towns have been denuded of their meaning, their history and their humanity – for such is the weight that ornament and art carries. But in Britain and the United States it is different: US cities look like temporary encampments around the air-conditioning plants; British cities have been gutted and rebuilt and look simply ugly. The lack of historical continuity, the lack of symbolism in contemporary design has made life drab.

Critics are busy proposing alternatives. Charles Jencks is strong among them. His writings – and his home – speak his

ABOVE *Part of the Summer Room; the painting is by Allen Jones and it is based in part on* A Dance to the Music of Time *by the painter Nicolas Poussin. The Sun chairs with their 'sunburst' backs are made from layered planes of MDF (medium density fibreboard).*

RIGHT *The decoration of the Sun Table is centred around a circle of flame colour; the wood grain is painted to resemble nebulae. The nine planets are painted on each of the table's legs.*

ABOVE *Storage units, again in MDF, are painted in a mottled burnt red to give the hue of an Indian summer. In perspective 'the decoration is meant to suggest three women carrying baskets of grapes on their heads.'*

OPPOSITE *View through the house looking south (away from the Winter Room) and into the Time Garden. The large window is motorised and drops down to open up a view across the grounds framed theatrically by great swathes of curtain.*

mind. This is Charles Jencks' Thematic House in London. The American architect and critic has created it from an 1840s house in Holland Park. He and his wife, Maggie Keswick, explain in their book *Symbolic Architecture* that it is an attempt to face the question of meaning in an agnostic age.

In the past societies have shared common myths and common values – the Victorians, for example, built civic architecture which was embellished with sculpture and decoration that was drawn from Christianity, commerce, imperial conquest and civic pride. What are the comparable categories today?

Jencks and Keswick have adopted two clear strategies: in the search for content they have looked back in history to the development of human civilisation – the histories of the Egyptians, Greeks, Arabs, Jews, Chinese and Europeans. They have also taken some very simple but broadly understood human motifs – the four seasons, for example, is the clearest and one ideally suited to a decorative, thematic interpretation.

It is in many respects a deeply pretentious house, but pretentiousness need not mean fake – the architects are aware of the audacity of scale of some of their ideas. For example, you enter the house via an oval hall in which the idea of earth and sky and cosmos is used as a theme. It is a grand conception and Jencks and Keswick parody their own audacity by carrying the theme over into the cloakroom and lavatory – what they call the cosmic loo.

Some of the theme rooms work very well, especially where the symbolism is simple. The Winter Room is on the ground floor: it faces north, is warm and is dominated by a pagan God of fire – the head is based on that of Eduardo Paolozzi, artist and owner of a face which is in the mould of a pugilistic Roman Emperor. Jencks has recreated a sense of the atmosphere which is found in the paintings of 17th-century Dutch interiors. That is to say, the darks as well as the lights glow gorgeously.

This house is essentially good-hearted. Jencks and Keswick

LEFT *The Cosmic Oval – the entrance hall with a mural painted by William Stok. The figures represent free thinkers from history. The sentence around the top of the doors says: 'The cosmic law is/ time's rhythm which/ rules sun and moon/ the four seasons too/ giving heat and light/ over all architecture/ Egypt and China begin/ Archetypes and readymades/ the foursquare motif/ windows on the world/ the five building arts/ in free classic style/ twenty-two faces/ an eclectic whole/ of personal signs/ owls, lilies, cats/ fix a place in time.'*

ABOVE *The Solar Stair, physical and psychological centre of the house, with black hole by Eduardo Paolozzi.*

have been concerned to use different surfaces to bounce or absorb light and hence use it to model the space rather than simply fill it. However, very little of the design feels three-dimensional. This is almost a painter's or a graphic designer's house. There is no carving and most 'textures' are painted-on. Charles Jencks's designs tend to read as flat elevations rather than appear roundly as felt forms, a consequence of his using planes of wood and layering them. This is most evident in the furniture – planes of layered quarter-inch wood.

There is an enormous amount to interest the eye but little to feed the fingers – or the ears. One of the virtues of using a range of materials with real weights and different masses is the different sounds they make when you touch them, walk on them, or put a glass down on them. If or when the architects move on to their next house, perhaps they will include stone and wood carvers, metalsmiths, even potters – experts who (few in number) understand the intelligence of materials.

RIGHT *The Spring Room – with busts of April, May and June.*

BELOW *The Winter Room – 'old age, warmth, saturated colours and reading are traditionally associated with the coldest season.'*

BELOW RIGHT *The architectural library – 'a village of bookcases set beneath a blue, curved ceiling supposed to recall the London skyline at dusk.'*

LOPEX PLC

THIS IS THE RECEPTION of a marketing group. Advertising is one of Britain's great success stories and London is claimed as the world's centre of the 'industry'. Dubbed the 'want makers', the advertising world is regarded with a mixture of admiration and scepticism: admiration for the extreme cleverness of the images and words generated by the want factories, scepticism because advertising is regarded as a sleight of hand.

The role of advertising is to give prominence to good products, make more people want them and thus help to lower the price of things that we want. But so good are manufacturers at making things – be it lager or cars – that there is very little material difference between one brand or one manufacturer and another. However, competition greases the engine of capitalism and so we need the 'hidden persuaders' to make pretences that there are differences worth buying. It is an exciting and creative art and the bright graduates of the Universities of Oxford and Cambridge, who might have been writing novels, scripting films or producing tedious moralising plays, are year by year attracted to making adverts. And making money. The money is good.

The knock-on effect of the advertisers' creativity has been felt in architecture, interiors, product and graphic design – all these activities have been forced to be cleverer, wittier and show more front to the public than hitherto. After the Second World War the various design professions were filled with utilitarian ideals but by the 1980s everyone had followed the designers of television and cinema commercials into the business of meeting, teasing and, in a sense, attempting to seduce the public.

The British, of course, have long been known for having made a fine art of hypocrisy: it is one reason why we still have a 'Rolls Royce' diplomatic service – hypocrisy is, in truth, a tool of self-improvement. We pretend that we are wonderful, then get so puzzled and feel so let down by the disparity between reality and fiction that eventually we set to and make the reality come a bit closer to the dream. This is especially true of the public services: year by year we have seen one public service after another advertise itself beautifully and then try to live up to its image. Currently struggling is British Rail.

The architecture and design of the premises inhabited by advertising agencies has to be impressive – it must look like the setting of a successful company. And, as has been noted elsewhere in this book, the reception area is especially important. You need a lot of front. This is it. The selling has begun as soon as you reach the reception desk. Perhaps that is why this interior looks so much like a contemporary shop.

LEFT *Reception desk. Note the glass clock. The design imagery here owes itself to the Russian Constructivists of the 1920s.*

ABOVE LEFT *One of the revolutions in the interior design of the last decade has been the substantial* improvement in lighting. The use of tinted glass offers a semi-opaque view into the other offices.

ABOVE RIGHT *Detail of one of the wall lamps.*

OPPOSITE *General view of the reception and public meeting area.*

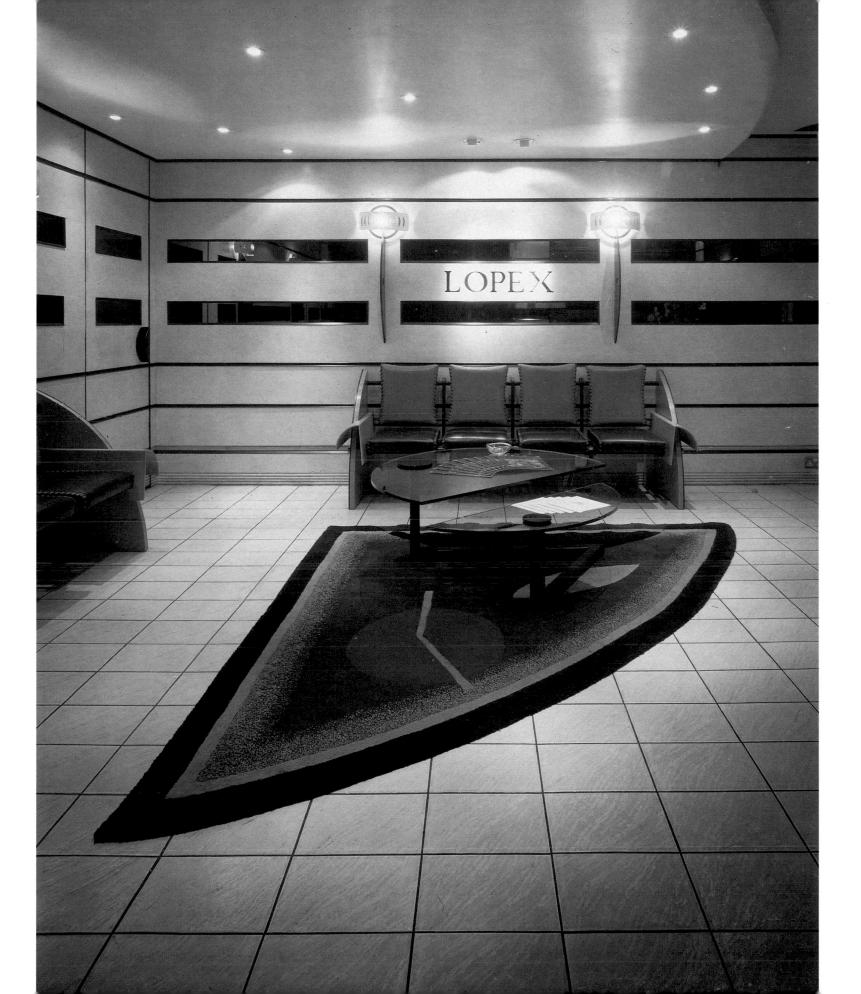

BLACKBURN HOUSE

THE FURNITURE IN Blackburn House – as in Charles Jencks' house (see page 198) – is clamorous in drawing attention to itself. Unlike the approach adopted by Jencks (which makes great use of painted, 'artificial' surfaces) the work accumulated by David and Janice Blackburn emphasises natural materials and real textures. There is a direct line between the work shown here and that of the Arts and Crafts movement of the early 20th century.

The self-consciousness of this interior – it is carefully composed, set and lit like an art gallery – is no more (and no less) elaborate than the self-consciousness we see in the Adam interiors (see page 23). It is through homes such as these that we are able to appreciate how the home becomes an act of self-expression. How does it differ from other examples of self-assertiveness in this book, such as the Tower House by William Burges (see page 172)? First, the Blackburn interior is very much plainer – there is the appearance of decoration but in fact it is very subdued and curtailed. This means that the overall composition is simpler to organise; there are plenty of plain walls and a bare floor against which a length of simple texture can be juxtaposed. Look, for example, at the fin radiators against the wall. The contrast and play-off between the finned cylinder and the plain wall is very pleasant.

Equally, we see simple geometric forms played off against simple organic ones – look at the swirling rug against the geometric sofa. This is an interior of formal flower arranging, modern in that very little of the content is figurative and most of it is flat, two-dimensional and graphic. Not *literally* two-dimensional – you can, after all, sit on the furniture – but it tends to be built up in planes, a construction rather than a rounded

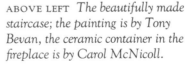

ABOVE LEFT *The beautifully made staircase; the painting is by Tony Bevan, the ceramic container in the fireplace is by Carol McNicoll.*

ABOVE RIGHT *The chair is in bleached maple and was designed by an American, Bob Trotman. Why it should look like the big gut is no doubt one of those post-modernist ironies that designers, stylists and architects like to chat about between themselves over supper.*

LEFT *In the foreground there is a desk by Floris van den Broecke, Professor of Furniture Design at the*

Royal College of Art; the small yellow sculpture is by Allen Jones. The delicious run of cupboards is in sycamore veneer.

OPPOSITE *Bob Trotman also designed the table in the hall, made in birds-eye maple and worked on with cuts and burn marks. The double-height glass windows were designed by Peter Wilson. The overall opacity excludes an unpleasant view whilst the little rectangles of transparency allow you to keep a weather eye open.*

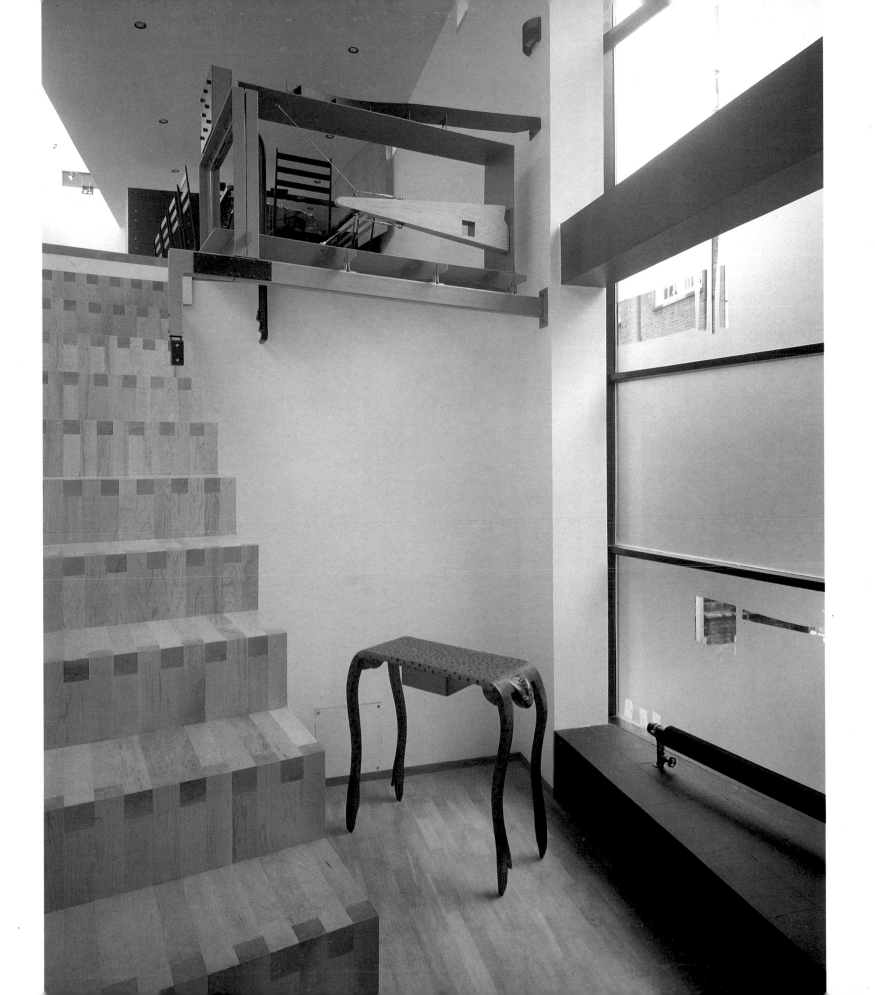

form. And what figurative work there is, such as the Andy Warhol portraits, is mechanistic or flattened, as in Bob Trotman's table.

Burges's house, on the other hand, is filled with figures and with rounded modelled or carved work. One of the great changes between 1889 and 1989 is the modern fixation on assemblage and construction – carving and modelling are all but gone in the modern interior. The other great difference between most avant garde interiors now and those of the late 19th century (Jencks excepted) is colour.

One of the successes of Blackburn House is its lighting and its variety of vistas and perspectives. The lighting is very nicely done and is enhanced by the variety of surfaces in each room: dull or painted metal, polished (but not over polished) wood, plaster, glass and fabric. The different ways in which these different materials reflect and absorb light plays an important role in the modelling of space.

The architects for this interior, a home within the building which also houses David Blackburn's office, were the Wilson Partnership and Chassay Wright. David is a property developer; Janice runs the Saatchi Gallery in North London.

ABOVE RIGHT *The wall sculpture is called* Sidestep, *by Michael Craig-Martin – a conceptual artist who came to public prominence with a glass of water which he called an oak tree – a demonstration of the philosophical possibilities attendant on meaning, intention, and wishful thinking.*

RIGHT *The appliqué-work bedspread by Susan Maxwell is a charming relief in an austere room.*

OPPOSITE *The ash slat chair visible in the distance is by the American sculptor Scott Burton; the settee is by Jasper Morrison, one of Britain's most talented young designers. The floor covering uses a popular 1980s device of marking out the space and suggesting a route through the interior. The paintings are of the Blackburns' sons and are by Andy Warhol, following his now famous format developed in the silkscreened series of Marilyn Monroe.*

NIGEL COATES' FLAT

WHEN A GROUP of young, London-based architects gave themselves the acronym NATØ there was some perplexity among journalists. The perplexity gave way to confusion when it was learned that NATØ stood for *Narrative Architecture Today*. Although he modestly insists on the other members of the group being noticed, the prime mover, as far as the public is concerned, is Nigel Coates: architect and designer.

Narrative architecture means, as you would expect, architecture that tells a story. NATØ so intended that its architecture should not be destructive and should, instead, make do with what there is. NATØ wanted a democratic architecture which always tolerated and often celebrated the idiosyncratic.

NATØ began in the early 1980s at the very point when Britain seemed in absolute decline – manufacturers were closing down across the country; the number of unemployed people increased hugely; large areas of the country, including the London docklands, lay waste. Coates and his colleagues observed that the hardware and processes of the industrial revolutions of the late 19th and early 20th century had finally broken down. Everywhere there were buildings and machinery that were too old to compete with the new machinery and peculiarly disciplined social infrastructures of Japan and Taiwan. So what to do with all the debris?

The obvious answer is (as the docklands have shown) to throw it all out and begin again. But in a laterally thinking move NATØ said why not leave things more or less as they are and just tweak them a bit? If a building is disused then convert it to another, community use, but not with too much fresh paint or new things (too costly, too bureaucratic). NATØ advocated recycling lumps of concrete, packing cases and corrugated sheet into furniture, doors or light fittings and proposed linking buildings with walkways and creating theme areas. In his ArkAlbion show Coates suggested turning out the bureaucrats from County Hall, in those days still the bastion of the Greater London Council, and putting them on barges on the Thames. County Hall would thus be freed for more useful functions.

Many of the plans were given life through Coates' extraordinary and beautiful drawings but clearly they had no chance at all of being put into practice. Planners loathe 'untidiness'. Today, Coates is teamed up with Doug Branson, another architect, and together they have a successful architectural firm – Branson Coates. It is one of the genuinely inventive firms in Britain.

OPPOSITE *Looking through from the dining room lies the NATØ globe in which the Surrey Docks take up much of the Northern hemisphere (NATØ was concerned with them at the time, 1983). There stands also a photograph of a Piranesi candelabra. There is another at the other end of the flat.*

LEFT *Venetian mirror – a tourist knick-knack from the 19th century, recovered in a Glasgow antique shop. The bottles on the glass shelf contain Moroccan pigments; one contains Saharan sand.*

BELOW *A corner of the Aerodrobe – for hanging clothes. This was a project done for NATØ living rooms.*

RIGHT *Spider lights done in 1986, part of a group of light fittings that can be done to order.*

BELOW LEFT *The famous sanded door – it was a picture of this door which got Coates his Japanese clients. The column of the giant candle was rescued from a skip and married to a flame lamp.*

BELOW RIGHT *A painting by Adam Lowe (1985) called Vanitas; it contains, as still-lifes of the genre do, a skull ... a reminder that 'our little life is rounded by a sleep'.*

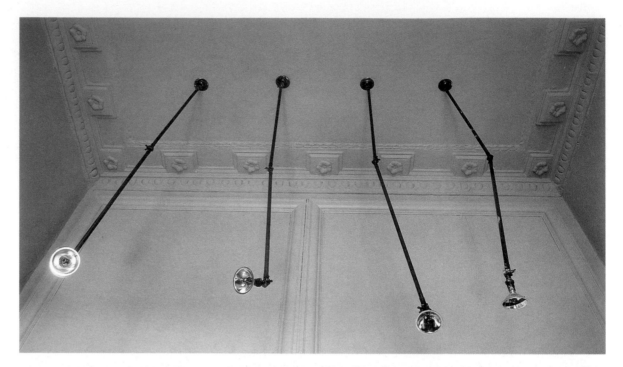

UNILEVER HOUSE

UNILEVER IS VAST; worldwide it employs nearly 300,000 people. It manufactures foods and detergents and has other interests including speciality chemicals and agribusiness feeds. Like all major corporations it offers a world within a world; there is a corporate identity, it needs to maintain a company ethos. People can build their lives with the company.

And, as befits a major corporation, all aspects of its public and private identity including its major offices must promote the idea that the company is responsible and cares about quality. The London headquarters of Unilever – Unilever House – was completed in 1932 and art historians describe its imposing facade as the result of a conflict between wanting a historical and classical style but demanding, at the same time, large office spaces. The building, a prominent landmark overlooking Blackfriars Bridge, now houses 1250 staff.

Unilever House was designed by J. Lomax Simpson and Sir John Burnet (the latter also designed the King Edward VII Galleries of the British Museum). Today the building, which has been added to, has 450,000 square feet of floor space. The new North Wing was designed with modern , electronic and information technology services in mind.

The headquarters have been completely refurbished as an Art Deco show piece. So successful was this that Unilever won a City Heritage award; moreover the refurbished building has become one of the most quoted examples of the 'art in public places' movement.

Working with Unilever on the refurbishment was Theo Crosby, a principal in Pentagram, one of Britain's leading design studios. He initiated what is regarded as one of the most extensive commissioning of art and craft projects of recent decades in the refurbishment of the building's interior.

Theo Crosby has campaigned passionately for architects to help the late 20th-century revival of decorative art skills and fine art skills by employing artists and craftsmen. Crosby is thus a leading voice for art in public places, arguing that there should be a legal requirement that one per cent of the construction cost of a building be given over to embellishment.

Historically, all the way from the Parthenon to the building of St Peter's in Rome, more was spent on decorating a public building than constructing its shell. With regard to St Peter's Basilica the ratio was about 50:50. No one could afford such ratios today but Unilever has made a considerable effort.

TOP *Inside lift panels designed by Eric Gill. The decoration depicts different forms of modern travel, hence the streamlined racing car. The sea, sun, moon and stars motif suggests travel by sea and air.*

ABOVE LEFT AND RIGHT *The outside lift panels are new but they incorporate Gill's designs.*

OVERLEAF *The ornate moulded plasterwork of the entrance hall ceiling was designed by Theo Crosby and based on Art Deco patterns.*

The original building and the newer North Wing are connected by a central entrance hall and the style is a modern version of Art Deco, the geometrical, brightly coloured fashion of the 1930s. Unilever House has a large art collection – it is a part of the policy and image building of the company to support fine art. Not all of it is contemporary. There is a varied collection of traditional artefacts collected from around the world which act as 'reminders' of the company's worldwide interests (it has activities in more than 70 countries).

The extent of the art thus runs from fibreglass sculptures of contemporary idiom to religious carvings from the Philippines and Eskimo carvings from Canada.

All the public areas and the corridors of the building are decorated with paintings, tapestries and sculptures. There are various practical reasons for this approach. Apart from the image conveyed to the public of a *caring* company, an important factor given the vulnerability of multinationals to the accusation that they are both anonymous and self-centred, the creation of a creative environment does show *employees* that the management is thoughtful – this matters very much. Art is thus used as an emollient.

ABOVE RIGHT *Looking down the stairwell from the sixth floor. Standing on plinths in each marble recess between floors are the maquettes of the statues, created by Nicholas Munro, that were commissioned during the renovation programme to be placed on the exterior at the new eighth floor level (the level that replaced the original blind attic on the façade).*

RIGHT *The entrance floor is marble, and the reception desk timber. The staircase balustrade is bronze with coloured decorative motifs. The company's international spread of activities is suggested by the many gifts from Unilever companies around the world that adorn various parts of the building. Seen here is a hollow cast by Nata Raja, depicting the dancing god Shiva, given by Unilever Hindustan.*

THE CLORE GALLERY

THE PUBLIC ROWS that accompanied the design and opening of James Stirling's Clore Gallery at the Tate in 1987 were hugely enjoyable, especially the arguments over the colour of the walls on which the paintings – all by Joseph Turner (1775-1851) – were to be hung. Turner is regarded as Britain's most important painter.

James Stirling has an international reputation as an important architect. Two famous Stirling buildings, the Engineering Faculty building in Leicester, and the History Faculty Building (Cambridge University) have both influenced architectural style and been heavily criticised for their lack of durability. Stirling's other famous building is the *Staatsgallerie*, Stuttgart – it has won almost universal praise. The Clore Gallery, funded by six million pounds given by the daughter of Sir Charles Clore, has been both loved and despised.

The Clore Gallery, which the lay public insist on calling the Turner Gallery, was bound to be controversial because Turner's will was so muddled. Turner left his 'finished' pictures to the National Gallery and he left money for the erection of a gallery to house them. But Turner's relatives disputed the will and after four years' legal wrangling the National Gallery ended up with all the work in the estate, including drawings and sketchbooks, while the relatives had all the money. The National Gallery was never given the means to fulfil Turner's bequest. Some paintings went to the Tate and the drawings to the British Museum.

In 1975, Turner's bicentennial, the Turner Society was formed to fight for a national gallery dedicated to Turner. And with the Clore Gallery's opening in 1987 the Society has more or less got what it wanted after fighting a very popular public campaign.

Stirling's choice of colour has caused comment. The acidic pastels either give the entrance and stairway a spirit of lighthearted welcome or a yobbish seaside rock vulgarity. You choose. The galleries are criticised by some for not having enough colour. One argument declares that the Victorian taste for hanging paintings on, say, crimson flocked paper, is sounder than hanging paintings on light-coloured walls. White walls bounce the light back and make it harder to see the paintings; dark walls allow the paintings to reflect the light.

WILLOW HOUSE

WITHOUT WISHING to make Brian Muller seem pretentious there is a sense in which he attempts to do to this interior what Bertold Brecht did to the theatre: which is to suspend illusion and bring structure into the forefront of our attention. What interests Muller is the idea of 'layering' – one's eye is arrested by, for example, a wall in the mid-distance, but the edge of the wall takes the eye a little further on to, say, a semi-opaque glazed door, and then on beyond to a window in the next room. The house opens up into a series of landscapes; always the eye is pulled outside but then the outside has been pulled in. This is a clever house.

In the old, Victorian part of the building, the original plaster ornamentations act like little pieces of text reminding you of the age of the building but the house is, in fact, embraced and enclosed by a carapace of glass and metal. The old is in tension with the new – but the tension is intellectual, not physical. Thus the mind is engaged but the body is not discomfited. That might sum up the art of good architecture.

One of Brian Muller's earlier houses is discussed on page 110. He is an architect who pulls and pushes each house he lives in into a reconfiguration around his own practical – and emotional – wants, as well as those of his family.

Willow House was originally a red brick end-of-terrace Victorian house with the side and rear walls taken out. There is a 'lean to' conservatory on the south-east wall and an enclosed pool/sauna in the back garden. An interesting outside/inside environ-

ABOVE *Metallic silver grey blinds are motorised and permit some fine control over the wallowing light.*

LEFT *The upper living area with Hans Coray's famous aluminium chairs in the foreground. The weep-*ing *fig tree softens the otherwise super-rational landscape.*

OPPOSITE *A watercolour play of light – daylight configures and reconfigures the house constantly like the ever-shifting light of the sea.*

ment has been created that reassesses usual assumptions.

To describe this as a 'high tech' house would be too tabloid and would imply a slavish commitment to one of the 1980s' emptier and soulless styles. But Muller enjoys the finesse of good engineering and the clean thinness of line that metal and glass provides. The effect is softened by little, knobbly visual jokes – such as the 'broken wall' (a didactic ornament, its layers of brick to plaster to painted plaster are a little history of the building's construction) and the plaster casts of Victorian ornaments mixed with the modern lights and stark shelving. In several respects this is a house of narratives – a 'literary' building which can be broken down into a variety of meanings.

BELOW *The revealed and 'broken' wall has been artfully finished to show its construction (we see each layer of the process). It is a light-hearted symbol of the old house and a very typical late 20th-century architectural device. In this century the collage approach to design has been triumphant: eclectism, found objects and juxtapositions are to our designers what careful carving, modelling and painting were to craftsmen of previous centuries.*

OPPOSITE *The pool has a black lining and with the light falling upon it the effect created is that of a deep, still tarn. It actually contains a wave machine so you can swim 'against the current'. The pink pipe has ducts which suck in the moist air and pump out dry warm air. This way the pool area is kept both warm and free of condensation.*

THE FRAME STORE

LONDON HAS BEEN HOST traditionally to tens of thousands of small businesses, workshops and studios. The trades and the crafts may change but small business thrives. In Soho, which has flourished on the crafts of selling sex and good food, there has been a recent expansion in media services – graphic design, television and film making.

The Frame Store is a post-production and film editing company in Soho; it is a 'facility house' where television commercials are edited. A particular specialism is the construction and editing of television graphics. The technology underlying this craft is highly sophisticated and uses state-of-the-art computer systems with homely names such as Paintbox and Harry.

Such equipment is expensive and space-consuming. Frame Store required three separate workspaces for each bank of computer and video consoles and another workspace for a huge computerised rostrum camera. Space was also needed for offices, a reception area, and a café for the employees – and it all had to be squeezed into a Victorian building of less than 4,000 square feet.

The budget for this enterpise was small – £70,000 – but with it the designer, Mark Kubaczka of Rodney Fitch and Company, has succeeded in creating a work base and a piece of visual propaganda for the young company.

Mark Kubaczka took his inspiration from the company's cor-

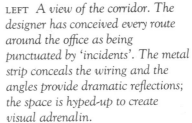

LEFT *A view of the corridor. The designer has conceived every route around the office as being punctuated by 'incidents'. The metal strip conceals the wiring and the angles provide dramatic reflections; the space is hyped-up to create visual adrenalin.*

ABOVE LEFT AND RIGHT *Each door and architrave was designed by Kubaczka to mark out spaces and functions. These are the toilet and shower rooms. The bright, brittle yellow figures are designed to suggest edginess and energy.*

porate identity, the designs that they were already using in their advertising and publicity material. The company's corporate identity is rather 1950s in flavour – the predominant colours are turquoise, red, yellow and black, and the company motif is a thing that looks like a flying saucer (and flying saucers are definitely 1950s).

Design-orientated companies like to have a lot of front. They believe that providing as much space as possible for the reception area and filling that space theatrically to create a drama is money well spent. In the Frame Store reception area, the money has been spent on a dominating 'sculpture' based on the flying saucer logo. Once again, we see design's indebtedness to contemporary art – the sculpture owes its pedigree to Philip King and Anthony Caro (two well-known British abstract sculptors in metal).

It is interesting that the overall effect of flattened coloured planes is derived, albeit circuitously, from the abstract art of the Dutch and the Russians of the 1920s – work which has had a great influence on graphic design in the post-Second World War period. Other influences are at work here too, including Pop Art, which in its turn fed off graphic design – in this century design has become like a rugby match with a ball of relatively few ideas being passed back and forth or seized and made off with. The decorative art of interior design, like all applied art, is only as good as the art of its century and generally lags behind it by 20 years or more.

One of the more subtle touches in an understandably brash and perhaps relatively temporary decor, is the use of different floor finishes to signify and direct the visitor to the separate parts of the office.

ABOVE *The entrance to the conference room and, at the far end, the red doors announcing the entrance to the café.*

RIGHT *The large, three-dimensional interpretation of the company's flying saucer motif is made from MDF (medium density fibreboard), a material beloved by designers because, although it is expensive and horribly heavy, it can be cut and planed with ease and provides a good surface on which to paint.*

THE ISMAILI CENTRE

T HE CULTURAL CLUSTER of South Kensington museums – Science, Natural History, and the Victoria and Albert – has been enriched by the beautifully made Ismaili Centre. This centre, not itself a museum, sits on an island site opposite the V&A. It is a spiritual and social focus for the Shia Ismaili Muslim community.

Designed by the Casson Conder Partnership, the building brings to the fore the importance of the Islamic tradition in architecture, ensuring that it takes its proper place alongside the Greek, Roman, Byzantine and Gothic traditions celebrated in the buildings nearby.

The foundation stone was laid in 1979 by Lord Soames in the presence of the Aga Khan, the Imam or leader of the Ismailis who, with his brother, was responsible for approving everything about the new building. This is the first such specially commissioned building for the Ismaili Community in the West.

The Ismaili centre is exquisite in its detailing and its craftsmanship. And, of course, the quality of the workmanship has had a sound base in the excellence of the materials used. There is a clear reciprocity between outside and inside created by the consistent use of polished granites, bevelled glass and teak wood.

Inside, the heart of the building is the large prayer hall on the second floor which presents a gentle climax to a rippling progression of foyers and staircases. The entrance areas on the ground floor are designed to absorb a lot of people quickly, but the outer hall is intended to encourage a gradual dispersal of people. Such well-mannered crowd control by design is necessitated by the sites being bounded by very heavy traffic and relatively narrow pavements.

Traditional Islamic designs have inspired much of the detailing: for example, there is the calligraphy, here stylised and abstracted, and a numerical symbolism which has also been worked into the designs. More general 'Islamic' features include the use of honeycombing, glazed tiling, pierced screens and mirrorwork. Throughout the building the spaces are linked by a formal geometry of inlaid or painted lines – the goal is to achieve a symbol of unity.

The building has its secrets. The top floor has its rooms arranged in an open courtyard containing an outstanding roof garden. The integration of interior with exterior spaces is an Islamic tradition but the building as a whole is not a pastiche.

TOP *The doors leading from the outer entrance hall to the interior social, religious and administrative areas. The doors are Burmese teak.*

ABOVE *The outer entrance hall. The calligraphy, in relief on the wall facing the entrance doors, reads, 'In the name of Allah, the* compassionate, the merciful.' It is a preface to readings in the Koran.*

OPPOSITE *The ceiling design in the inner (main) entrance hall was done by Karl Schlamminger, a German Ismaili. The builders, Jonathan James Ltd, won a Guild of Plasterers award for this work.*

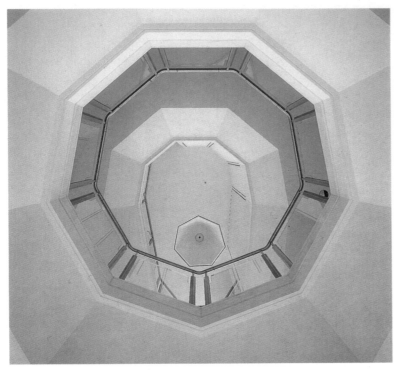

Islamic design has been dovetailed into Western style – a necessary metaphor for a community which retains its cultural identity whilst living in a host community with which it must exchange ideas and values as well as trade.

The Islamic religion, based on the teachings of the Arab prophet Muhammad (570-632), encourages rich, decorative arts as well as architectural language. The *Koran* prohibits cult images and representations of the Prophet and other holy persons. However, as with all old and complex religions, there are disagreements with regard to what the faithful may or may not include in their decoration. Some Muslims hold that any naturalistic painting or carving (including that of leaves and flowers) is blasphemous.

The tendency has thus been to produce an art which is stylised, geometric, and abstract. The result has been that a system of idealised, contemplative rather than combatative art has emerged. And one of the great flowerings of Islamic art is calligraphy, a craft which the West regards, to its cost, as minor.

Without an art of naturalistic illusion and a concentration upon the geometric and the patterned, it is unsurprising that

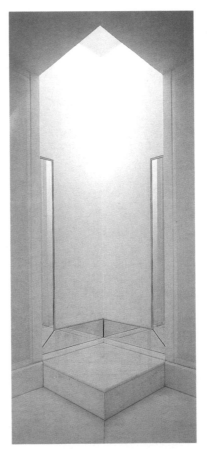

ABOVE LEFT *The geometry of the balconies on the two upper floors. The staircase handrail is made from stainless steel, edged with brass. The banisters are plate glass. Where each flight of stairs begins and ends there are dimples and returns in the handrails to inform the blind.*

FAR LEFT *One of the lift halls which has fixed teak seating, and also the blue recessed painted lines and the white marble flooring which is used throughout the building.*

LEFT *A decorative display niche. It is lit from above to highlight the textures and inlays. The geometry of this niche shows in one small particular the abstracted idealism sought by the interior as a whole.*

Islamic art developed a heightened sensitivity towards materials. It also takes pleasure in the sensuous aspects of surface.

In the Ismaili Centre traditional and modern materials have been juxtaposed: white marble, blue Brazilian granite and stainless steel is one example. The designs are chords of lustres – the Ismaili Centre has no surfaces that bounce the light hard back at you; it is all modulated.

From outside, the building seems introspective, the windows appear small, but inside we see that the light penetration is artful and more than sufficient. The artificial lighting is uniformly excellent; much of it is directed from concealed fittings in order to maintain an ethereal atmosphere and create the kind of space in which sounds can be exploited as well as textures. Far too many modern interiors rely on ersatz material which look all right but have no resonance. Here the variation from carpet to stone to wood flooring provides a melodious aural texture.

Everything is brought into the whole. For example, by making the benches constructions of slats and rods, the theme of perforated, light architecture is maintained. There is strength throughout but no loud assertiveness. It is an interior of sweetness.

ABOVE RIGHT The corridor on the top floor has windows on the side opposite to the bench. The corridor runs around and overlooks the roof garden. Sound and light determine tranquillity: careful use of running water has been made in the garden and a planting scheme based on blue and white hues increases the communion between outside and inside. The garden was designed by the late Lanning Roper and Sasaki Associates. Beyond the corridor there is a multi-purpose divisible space which can be re-configured for small or large meetings as required.

RIGHT One of the eight bays in the social hall. Secondary glazing provides insulation from the horrid traffic noise of Cromwell Road and the bevelled glass in the panes diffuses the light. In the winter a mixture of uplighters and ceiling lights produces a warm, pinkish glow. The floor is made of North American oak and the furniture was designed or chosen by members of the UK Ismaili Community.

THE AUERBACH/LUCE HOME

CRUCIAL DESIGN has a very 1980s pedigree (see also page 150). In the beginning Kitty Bowler had a pine stripping business, and Joshua Bowler was a builder.

Kitty started making interior designs for property developers, and Joshua was involved with *Mutoid Waste*, a group of 'artists' who created recycled, fragmented temporary stage sets for warehouse parties – parties that were immensely popular as a part of the underground young London scene. The general style that emerged from these entrepreneurial initiatives is sometimes referred to as 'post-holocaust chic' – the sort of scene where, after the bomb has dropped you still have the wit, the style and the nous to mix a dry martini. Britons, especially Londoners, even young Londoners, have this nostalgia for *blitzed* landscapes. We like the look of a good war.

Kitty and Joshua Bowler opened a gallery in Notting Hill Gate. Naturally some of the artists they had associated with in the 'Warehouse' scene became prominent in the gallery. The gallery became inundated with artists. In fact the Bowlers had intended to open an interior design shop and it was some time before the first interior design commissions came through the gallery.

The partnership, although focused upon interior design, is rooted in ideas about contemporary art and the Bowlers have launched a programme of *Contemporary Art Auctions*. These have been devised to help aspiring artists reach a buying audience, and provide a non-selective forum for new work. At the same time the base of the buying audience has to be broadened and the Bowlers are trying to attract people for whom buying original art is strange and new.

Art is also big business – it is a huge industry which needs big amounts of work to keep the engines going. The success of initiatives such as those taken by the Bowlers is part of a late 20th-century phenomenon in the 'explosion' of art. There are more artists working in London today than in the whole of Renaissance Italy. And *Art In America*, one of the leading international art magazines, has commented that 'artists may fade and even the market itself may rise or fall with the state of the economy. But the art-marketing system is secure.'

It is arguable that the creation of a mass market in art occurred in the 1960s when popular music and the graphics it generated (posters, record album sleeves and the like) threw up new images which fed into 'mainstream' painting and sculpture. The father of populism in art was Andy Warhol; he was also one of the fathers of the new business of art – he turned 50-cent cookie jars into $1,000 art-e-facts; a new generation turns car fenders into 'art'. The popular base for the kind of art dealt in by the Bowlers is rooted in pop music rather than fine art history.

The Bowlers' quieter side is revealed here in the home of Jonathan Auerbach and Anne Luce. The wall finishes are

FAR LEFT *General view of the main living area. The sofa is by Ros Mortimer and the walls are gesso – white plaster and size – with painted water-colour on top which has then been sealed.*

LEFT *The staircase, designed and made by Joshua, is set off by some of his innovative wall finishing, a form of demur aurora borealis.*

OPPOSITE *The car seat is by Robin Cooke and the rug by Sue Saunders. The overall effect with so much literal and figurative imagery is faintly unsettling. A tribal art has been concocted out of Western artefacts and attitudes: it amounts to a peculiar perspective.*

interesting, and surface treatments have become a speciality of Joshua Bowler. The popularity of original surface finishes was given a boost in the early 1980s by the Italians. The Memphis design studio, a group of like-minded designers working in Milan, produced a number of designs for furniture, wall coverings and textiles that had highly elaborated 'abstract' surfaces.

At the time people thought that Memphis was a new breakthrough but wiser heads demurred and pointed out that what the Italians had re-invented was American working class style of the 1950s – a style that had flourished through popular demands for lively forms, colour and cheap glitziness. Thirty years later the style was rediscovered and recycled via Italian intellectuals and promoted through the colour supplements of Western Europe. It was an OK way of getting away from white walls without having to follow the very non-OK route of William Morris and Laura Ashley which was favoured in the late 1970s.

Here, of course, there are all kinds of checks and balances in the design. The composition of plain versus elaborated is artful enough not to overwhelm the rooms – always the mistake of working class homes in the 1950s.

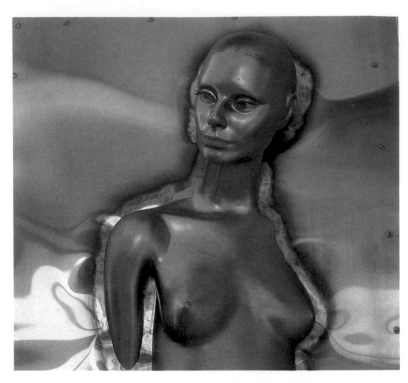

ABOVE *This sculpture by Robert Lee is a piece of true post-modernist hedging of bets – quasi-ethnic, quasi-figurative and a dash of the surreal.*

ABOVE RIGHT *A sculpture commissioned from Robin Cooke after the clients had seen the pieces in the 2000 Club (see page 150). This android look became fashionable in the late 1980s' television advertising.*

RIGHT *The automobile grille is from a Jaguar motorcar and is, in fact, a radio. The less than androgynous chairs were designed by Kitty Bowler and made by Joshua. The twin paintings are of Jon and Anne.*

SENATE HOUSE

THE SENATE HOUSE of the University of London has always had mixed reviews. To some it is a building of rare architectural integrity. To others it seems almost Stalinist in its massiveness and anonymity. The exterior is certainly forbidding. The interior, though hardly biddable, has a graciousness that comes as a relief.

Charles Holden (1875-1960) designed the building in 1931 and it is clearly a development of the design he created for London Transport's headquarter offices at No 55 Broadway (1927-29). The structure inside the main tower allows for changing the arrangement of rooms, and the steel-beamed floors were designed to be moved up and down. Whatever one thinks of the harshness of the building Holden was a very thoughtful architect. He was conscious of how his buildings would weather and he clearly anticipated the inevitable effects of London's pollution and England's weather.

Holden had a long, extremely fruitful association with London Transport and he was responsible for many of the Underground stations on the outer reaches of the Piccadilly lines. These brick and glass structures are uncompromising in their geometry, but the entrance halls are very generous in their height, with windows reaching the full way to the roof. Holden created interiors that are light and airy as well as cathedral-like. Such buildings would not be created today; today the style might be a faked-up cheesecake vernacular.

Holden was a classical architect, as his buildings such as Rhodesia House (originally commissioned by the British Medical Association, 1907-1908) clearly show; but his design for the Senate House leaves a geometrical essence without any temporising elegance. Holden led the architectural avant garde; he was a friend of Jacob Epstein, the sculptor, and commissioned sculpture from him to adorn the BMA building (Rhodesia House). There was a public outcry at Epstein's naked bodies – the sculptures were eventually removed.

LEFT *If the Senate building en masse is Stalinist, the details, nonetheless, are very beautiful – as with this simple, well-proportioned door.*

OVERLEAF *Holden had developed the uplighter in his design work for London Transport and here they are used to great effect. The atmosphere created by Holden's lighting is extraordinary – it is so Roman, so 'ideal' in its lack of concession to human individuality. An awesome beauty.*

RIGHT *Beautiful, symmetrical trimmings adorn an otherwise austere interior.*

BELOW *The formal simplicity is intense and intimidating but the obvious play-off in geometry, the rectangles versus the half-circles, is beautiful. Note the detailing – the lipped steps and the architrave to the doors.*

BELOW *Holden's use of classical proportion is clearly evident here – and what is impressive is his sense for the ceremonial. This is real grandness, not just theatre. Very high quality materials are used with travertine marble for the floors and walls.*

TOWNSEND'S HOUSE

OULD MODERNISM, the style of the 20th century, be due for a reassessment or, even, a revival? During the 1980s modernism was reviled – and understandably so. The 1970s ended in a chorus of criticism at the obvious failures in the modern idiom – concrete architecture that no-one wanted to work or live in, and systems-built buildings in which the rain flowed on the inside as well as the outside of the windows. Tastes are fickle however, for only 20 years ago Victorian Gothic was reviled but, as evidenced in this book, it has now since been rehabilitated.

Therefore it is a pleasure to see a family home which has kept faith with the best in the modern style. For what we see in the Townsend's House (designed by John Townsend in 1974) is the combination of simplicity, lightness and spaciousness which, in its overall atmosphere, is comparable with Georgian space.

One of the features of this home is clearly the use made of the inside/outside relationship – one of the most potent of all architectural recipes. The sloping glass wall creates a *frisson* of delight by defining what in most homes is invisible – the frontier between security, warmth and peace and the rest of the world. This boldly engineered interface is an architectural metaphor for that delicious sensation of being securely wrapped in bed whilst outside the cold rain lashes at the window.

Much use has been made of good quality materials and a part of the building's success is due to the interplay between plants and the garden and the concrete, glass and plaster-faced walls. In a sense this exposes another age-old recipe – understood by Women's Institute flower arrangers, architects and Japanese gardeners alike – the 'compare and contrast chords' that are created by off-setting smooth with textured, natural with unnatural surfaces, and organic with the obviously engineered. The predominance of white and yellow (there is a range of yellow hues in the wood) gives a sunny atmosphere in a Northern climate.

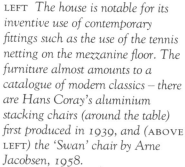

LEFT *The house is notable for its inventive use of contemporary fittings such as the use of the tennis netting on the mezzanine floor. The furniture almost amounts to a catalogue of modern classics – there are Hans Coray's aluminium stacking chairs (around the table) first produced in 1939, and (ABOVE LEFT) the 'Swan' chair by Arne Jacobsen, 1958.*

ABOVE RIGHT *The 'Gran Confort' chair designed by one of the fathers of modernism, Le Corbusier with Charlotte Perriand in 1928.*

OPPOSITE *This is a house with two lives. We are unused to domestic architecture transforming itself in public in this way: the opening out of the house to the night is very un-English. It is also a demonstration of private confidence.*

ED'S DINER

THIS IS A REPLICA OF 1950s American diners. Whenever one considers the 1950s in the USA one centres on three things: TV, Rock'n'Roll and the automobile. It was the automobile that dictated, and dominated, style – and what dominated the automobile was lots of swollen chrome. The style found itself transferred into fast food restaurants because the style symbolised up-to-dateness, success, speed and youth. It also came to symbolise cleanliness and good eating. One of the marketing successes of American fast food franchises was to raise the quality of fast food and lower its price.

Commentators have pointed out that a characteristic of 1950s US design is the predominance of shapes that look as though they ought to be put into the mouth and sucked. Fifties style is particularly appropriate to places of food consumption.

The development and consumption of fast food was a natural American development in a culture which has been described as restless and temporary. Even many of the cities look like temporary bivouacs, as though the greater part of the population is made up from itinerants. The 1950s was the decade when the great interstate freeways were built and transcontinental travel was made easy for the middle majority American.

The owner of Ed's Diner is Barry Margolis and he got the idea from his visits to the East Coast of America. He has set up three diners in London – in Soho, the Kings's Road and Hampstead. These cult-status, limited-edition outlets are another example of building as self-advertisement – but done with much greater elan than some native designs glimpsed at the sides of highways in Britain.

LEFT *The Coca-Cola machine is a restored 1950s original.*

ABOVE *The counter is the focus of the diner. The preparation and cooking of the food is done in front of the customer.*

RIGHT *The stools are adapted from customised bases, with thickened and squared seats.*

BELOW *No laminates are used in the kitchen, where stainless steel rules for hygiene.*

OVERLEAF *The juke-boxes are originals. The decor is in laminates using a modern Italian design which echoes the 1950 Memphis style.*

KEY TO EXTERIORS

HAYS GALLERIA
Tooley Street
Bermondsey SE21

THE HOOVER BUILDING
Weston Avenue
Perivale

TV-AM
Hawley Crescent
Camden Town NW1

CHARLES JENCKS' HOUSE
Notting Hill W11

LOPEX COMMUNICATIONS PLC
St Martin's Lane
Covent Garden WC2

BLACKBURN HOUSE
Hampstead NW3

NIGEL COATES' HOUSE
South Kensington SW7

UNILEVER HOUSE
Blackfriars
The City EC4

CLORE GALLERY, THE TATE
Millbank
Westminster SW1

WILLOW HOUSE
Hampstead NW3

THE FRAME STORE
Great Pulteney Street
Soho W1

THE ISMAILI CENTRE
Cromwell Road
South Kensington SW7

THE AUERBACH/LUCE HOME
Campden Hill
Holland Park W8

SENATE HOUSE
Malet Street
Bloomsbury WC1

THE TOWNSENDS' HOUSE
Camden Mews
Camden Town NW1

ED'S DINER
The King's Road
Chelsea SW3

Index

BIBLIOGRAPHY

BOOKS

Beard, Geoffrey, *The Work of Robert Adam*, Bloomsbury Books 1987

Clun, Harold, *The Face of London*, Simpkin Marshall 1932

Fleming, John and Honour, Hugh, *The Penguin Dictionary of Decorative Arts*, Penguin 1979

Hitchcock, Henry-Russell, *Architecture Nineteenth and Twentieth Centuries*, Penguin 1958

Jencks, Charles, *Towards A Symbolic Architecture*, Academy Editions 1985

Jones, Edward and Woodward, Christopher, *A Guide to The Architecture of London*, Weidenfeld and Nicholson 1983

Osborne, Harold (Editor), *The Oxford Companion to the Decorative Arts*, Oxford University Press 1986

Pevsner, Nikolaus, *London*, Volume One, Penguin 1972

Rasmussen, Steen Eiler, *London*, Cape 1958

Service, Alastair, *The Architects of London*, The Architectural Press 1979

Service, Alastair, *Edwardian Interiors*, Barrie and Jenkins 1983

CATALOGUES AND BROCHURES

ArkAlbion (NATØ), *Architectural Association* 1984

Business Design Centre Brochure, Business Design Centre 1987

Campbell, Zogolovitch, Wilkinson & Gough, Company brochure 1988

Debenham House, broadsheet published by the Richmond Fellowship

Freemasons' Hall, Sir James Stubbs and T. O. Haunch, the United Grand Lodge of England 1983

The Guildhall of the City of London, the Corporation of London

Inside Unilever House, Unilever plc 1986

The Islamic Cultural Centre, published by the Centre

Leighton House Museum, published by Leighton House Museum

Linley Sambourne House, Simon Jervis and Leonee Ormond, the Victorian Society 1987

Mansion House, H. Clifford Smith, The Corporation of London 1984

The Michelin Building, Wendy Hitchmough, Conran Octopus/Heinemann 1987

National Westminster Hall, National Westminster Bank plc

The Old Bailey, the Corporation of London/the Sidney Press Ltd 1975

100 Park Lane, its Past and Present, the Hammerson Group 1987

Royal Palaces, Olwen Hedley, Pitkin Pictorials Ltd 1982

Theatre Nights and Theatre Knights, A History of the Maybox Theatres, Maybox 1985

ARTICLES

Anon, *The Bride of Denmark Architectural Review*, December 1955

Anon, *Inside Outside House* (Brian Muller), Designers' Journal, July 1988

Fuller, Peter, *Towards a New Nature for the Gothic*, Art and Design, April 1987

Jones, Ronald, *The Bath at the New Club House* (RAC Club), The Royal Automobile Club Journal, March 1911

Lee, Marjorie, *The Dorchester Renaissance*, available Dorchester Public Relations

ACKNOWLEDGEMENTS

This book would not have been possible without the help and support of numerous friends, colleagues and organisations. In particular I would like to thank: Rachel Duffield who got the ball rolling. Peter Dormer for the knowledge and wit he brought to the text and to James Harrison for editing it. Philip Lord and Andy Smith for their care with the overall design. Alex Freeman, my assistant. Sue Sharpe for her constant help and encouragement. And Joanna Lorenz, my editor, for her support and enthusiasm in seeing it all through to successful completion.

I would like to say a special thank you to all the staff at Studio Workshop for their unstinting support and for supplying my Sinar P camera and Broncolor lighting, all of which performed with usual faultless consistency. To all the staff at Push One who processed all my colour films as well as providing advice and encouragement. And to Chas at Grove Hardy for processing and printing all the black and white pictures.

Of the numerous people and organisations who allowed me access to their property or assisted me in other areas I would like to thank: Marie Jackson of the British Library, Sylvia Jones at Lancaster House, the Department of the Environment, the Foreign and Commonwealth Office, the Corporation of London, the Palace of Westminster, the Victoria & Albert Museum, National Westminster Bank PLC, Chris Christodoulou of the Royal Albert Hall, the staff at Syon Park, Vicky Trentham and the staff at the Food Halls at Harrods, Granada Leisure Ltd, Westminster Abbey, the Royal Opera House Covent Garden, Sally Price at the Dorchester Hotel, the Central London Mosque, Lloyd's of London, the Royal Naval College Greenwich, Brenda Popplewell at Alexandra Palace, all the staff at Fred Cooke's Eel and Pie shop, the staff at Wyndham's and Whitehall Theatres, Paul Hamlyn and Sir Terence Conran, the Victorian Society, Sir John Soane's Museum, the Business Design Centre, Dennis Severs, Mike Adkins and staff at Thames Water Authority, the staff at the Blackfriar Public House, the London Borough of Hounslow, Express Newspapers, the Spitalfields Trust, British Rail Property Board, the Hammerson Property and Investment Trust, the Peer Group PLC, Peter Raymond of the Cabman's Shelter Fund, the staff and pupils of Westminster School, Lewis and Joan Lupton, Ted and Angie Briscoe, Frank Atkinson the Librarian at St Paul's Cathedral Library, Robert Palmer, Pia Eckart, Peter and Phyllida Riddell, Phil and Mary Sharpe, the Reform Club, Bill Beckett, Anthony Annis, Mick Hurd, Mirijana Winterbottom at the Chelsea Arts Club, the staff at the Architectural Press, the Champneys Club (London), the London Borough of Sutton, Stephen Jones at Leighton House, Diane Williams of the Richmond Fellowship, Mary and Julian Scott, Anna Tully, English Heritage, the staff at the Warrington Hotel, Perry Press, Mr and Mrs Hollamby, the Royal Automobile Club, All Saint's Church Margaret Street, the Greek Cathedral Aghia Sophia, the staff at the Club 2000, Jenny Hall, the staff at the Library and Museum of the Freemasons' Hall, Michelle Julian and the staff at the Ritz, the staff at Bill Stickers, the staff at Hays Galleria, Joshua and Kitty Bowler, John, Nikolai and Vladimir Eatwell, TV-AM, John and Lyn Townsend and family, the Tate Gallery, Nigel Coates, Unilever PLC, the Ismaili Centre, Sharon Read of Frame Store, the University of London, Charles Jencks and Maggie Keswick and Nan, Brian Muller, Patrick Wiseman, Jenny Every, Nigel Szembel, Lopex Communications, Bruce and staff at Rocket Restaurants, David and Janiee Blackburn, Kusum Haidar, Indar and Aruna Pasricha, Louise Nicholson and finally Katie and Luke Freeman.

John Freeman

Peter Dormer would also like to thank Jan Burney (Design Journalist), Mairi Duthie (Researcher), Jonathan Glancey (Architectural Journalist), and Jane Hughes of Design Analysis International Ltd.